WINNING EDGE

MIKE HUSSEY

WINNING EDGE

BEHIND THE SCENES OF ELITE CRICKET

Mike Hussey
with David Sygall

hardie grant books

I would like to dedicate this book to my late father, Ted,
who had a passion for coaching and helping others.
I hope this book can help many others with their passion in life.

Published in 2015 by Hardie Grant Books

Hardie Grant Books (Australia)
Ground Floor, Building 1
658 Church Street
Richmond, Victoria 3121
www.hardiegrant.com.au

Hardie Grant Books (UK)
5th & 6th Floor
52–54 Southwark Street
London SE1 1UN
www.hardiegrant.co.uk

A Cataloguing-in-Publication entry is available from the catalogue of the National Library of Australia at www.nla.gov.au
Winning Edge
ISBN 978 1 74270 896 6

Cover design by Luke Causby/Blue Cork
Typeset in 12.5/17 pt Adobe Garamond Pro by Cannon Typesetting
Cover image courtesy of JEWEL SAMAD/AFP/Getty Images

Printed by McPherson's Printing Group, Maryborough, Victoria

The paper this book is printed on is certified against the Forest Stewardship Council® Standards. FSC promotes environmentally responsible, socially beneficial and economically viable management of the world's forests.

Contents

Acknowledgements

I WOULD LIKE TO thank and acknowledge the efforts of David Sygall for his many hours of hard work, during a personally trying time for him and his family. Thank you to Hardie Grant for their continued support and to my family for their loyalty and support over many years. I would also like to acknowledge Martin Darviniza, who conceived the idea for this book.

Introduction

DURING MY FORMATIVE years of playing cricket I became convinced that every team's dressing room was pretty much the same. The old blokes would talk, the young blokes would listen and there were basic unwritten rules about how to celebrate wins and deal with losses. This perception only strengthened for me over years of club, first-class and international cricket, as that dynamic, with some small variations, came up time and again. But there was one dressing room, of all the hundreds I had been part of, that became etched in my mind as a striking example of how much cricket was evolving and the challenges this would bring. It got me wondering whether the game I grew up with, and love so dearly, would ever be the same.

The Chennai Super Kings had every reason to be bitterly disappointed one night in May 2009 at Wanderers Stadium in Johannesburg. After being pipped at the post in the final of the Indian Premier League (IPL) the previous year by the Rajasthan Royals, our strong side, which featured the likes of MS Dhoni,

Matthew Hayden and spin king Murali, was confident of going all the way. Instead, our campaign fizzled when we were soundly beaten in the semifinal by the Royal Challengers Bangalore. A loss is a loss and I have experienced plenty of them. But this was different. Far from being the usual scene, our losing dressing room quickly unravelled into a muddle of competing interests and attitudes.

It was the second season of the IPL and we had been contracted to clubs for the first three seasons before player trading was allowed, meaning our side was largely unchanged between 2008 and 2010. Despite spending only a small amount of time together in preparation, the continuity across three years gave us, I believed, a chance to create a spirited unit that would work together to achieve our best possible results. But, as I looked around the dressing room in the moments after that loss to Bangalore, I felt anything but a sense that we had all been pushing in the same direction.

From the players' booth I looked out at a deeply disjointed environment. In one corner there was a group of players in quiet conversation about what had gone wrong. 'Coulda, shoulda, woulda' was probably the gist of their chat. Elsewhere, the coaches were grumbling among themselves discussing life, the universe and who knows what. The guys who had not played that night were leaning back against the lockers looking very relaxed, most having a giggle and a muck around. Some guys were doing media and others were talking to friends or family while the team manager buzzed around, organising interviews, explaining who was on which flight, where to leave packed bags, and a million other things. It was a group of individuals in one room who seemed to me to have very different motives. It was anything but the kind of team environment I had become accustomed to. We needed an icebreaker to bring things to some kind of conclusion, and it came from one of the coolest cricketers I have ever met.

The reluctant superstar MS Dhoni never raises his voice, does not say much on the field and little more off it. He is more inclined to explain the specs on his latest favourite motorbike than give deep thoughts about tactics or techniques. But he became captain of India for a reason – when he does say something, it is well worth listening to and nearly always has a worthwhile effect. This turned out to be one such occasion. Dhoni must have sensed the disunity in the room and, without a hint of emotion, sent a very clear message about what he thought had been going on and what had to happen.

'Some people play for money', Dhoni said softly but with typical authority. 'Some want the women, the parties, the fame. Others play just because they love the game of cricket. I want every player here to go away from this tournament and work out why they play the game.' Dhoni said he expected everyone to be honest and open about their conclusions when they returned for the following season.

Dhoni's forthright message, to me, was visionary, as it encapsulated in a few sentences the changing landscape of world cricket. The club-based Twenty20 leagues bring together players from different countries and cultures, which is a wonderful thing. It provides many positive outcomes. However, it can no longer be taken for granted that everyone within a dressing room shares the same motivations.

Playing cricket for the love of it had always come naturally to me. The physical and mental challenges and the camaraderie of working towards a goal with your teammates was all I ever needed to push me towards being at my absolute peak. The rest – the parties, the money, the travel – is great. But, really, it was always just a bonus. The focus for me was consistently and overwhelmingly on becoming as good a cricketer as I could possibly be, as an individual and as a contributor to the teams I represented.

In this Chennai team there was no doubt that some players were more interested in partying than playing cricket. The effect was that several players in the squad felt as though they were wasting their time, if not being betrayed. Dhoni's message got straight to the point and summed up the situation. His words must have hit close to home for most people in the room because where once there was a messy hum there fell a stunned silence.

In the time since that night in Johannesburg I have pondered whether Dhoni's words had an explicit effect. But just due to his openness and honesty, I believe, the following season there was more trust between the players and more of a belief that we were a united group with a common goal. When there were things on your mind you could talk to the bloke next to you about them. If there were concerns you held about something within the team you could raise them at group meetings. All of a sudden it was acceptable to step out of your shell and engage with the team rather than just concentrate on what you had to do individually. I certainly felt very comfortable in that Chennai team the season after that semifinal exit. I related well to my teammates and felt I could say what I wanted and would not be persecuted for it. Of course, it is impossible to measure precisely the impact Dhoni's address had on us. But the fact is, we won the IPL the next season and then took out the Champions League. And we won the IPL the following year, too.

Honesty sessions are certainly nothing out of the ordinary in cricket dressing rooms. I have been in hundreds of them. And they are nearly always the same. Those old blokes would say, 'We've gotta work together! We've gotta train harder! We've gotta want it more!' and the young guys would nod with a mixture of fear and enthusiasm. It is a very generic and traditional message. But what MS Dhoni said that day was, I believe, very much the honesty session for the modern era.

In cricket today – as in life generally – there are so many more variables, so many extra pitfalls and distractions that can creep into the dressing room and onto the field, placing extra pressure on individual performance, team unity and, ultimately, results. Just in the time since I first played for Australia, in 2004, cricket has undergone enormous changes, tossing up unprecedented challenges and opportunities, not only for administrators and officials but also for current and future players. These challenges have changed the concepts of excellence and success and forced all of us to reconsider our priorities in the game. It is something MS Dhoni clearly recognised and perfectly expressed.

It feels like a lifetime ago that I wrote my first book, *Driven to Succeed*. Not so much because of the years that have passed since it was published in late 2007, but because of what has happened in that time, both personally and around the world of cricket. After making my Test debut in 2005 against the West Indies at the Gabba in Brisbane I had a magical run at the top level, and by the start of 2008 had scored seven centuries and had a batting average above 80. In *Driven to Succeed* I enjoyed sharing my experiences of how I had become successful to that point, discussing issues such as building confidence, working with different personalities, goal-setting and preparation – key aspects I had to learn and refine on my long path from being a flimsy little club cricketer in Perth to becoming a fully fledged Australian Test batsman. Yet I always knew that this dreamy stage of my career would eventually give way to tougher times, as I kept reminding the many journalists who seemed fascinated by my so-called 'Bradmanesque' batting average.

Sure enough, those times arrived in late 2008, after which I got a much more realistic experience of being an international cricketer. There were still many soaring highs but also deflating lows. I experienced public pressure, internal squabbles and media scrutiny. I had fitness concerns, injuries and selection dramas. Meanwhile, the relentless travel became increasingly taxing on my family, my cricket and me. There seemed so much more to contend with. It was a real test of discipline and strength, and a period in which, I believe, by analysing my own situations and those of the people around me, I learned more about myself and cricket than I had in my entire life before it. These are the sorts of lessons and experiences I want to share in this book.

There is a wonderful tradition of cricket literature dating back more than a century. But there are few, if any, manuals youngsters can refer to as they go about learning the modern game. When I was a kid I sometimes referred to a 'how to play cricket' book that Greg Chappell had produced, which talked all about technique. It helped me understand how to play a good back defence, cover drive and so on. However, despite the long apprenticeship I had after that, I soon discovered that there is no textbook or instruction manual for all the moving parts on the periphery of elite cricket. No one ever explained to me how to move smoothly between different teams and different forms of the game, how to adapt to different conditions in short spaces of time, how to stay fresh when constantly travelling, eating different cuisines and moving between different cultures. I did not know how to deal with the various coaches, captains and teammates I would have. No one prepared me for bad press or how to avoid problems dealing with the media. I wondered what to look for in a manager and why I needed one at all. When it came to other off-field temptations and distractions, such as nightlife – a potential minefield in the age of social media – it was very much a case of learning on the job. Not only was the cricket incredibly intense but the challenge to remain focused, disciplined and dignified was perhaps just as tough. It felt like everyone wanted a piece of me but there was no reference point to turn to.

You might expect international cricketers to have these sorts of things worked out. But my experience was that this was not the case at all. Cricketers are not great communicators at the best of times and there is sparse, if any, discussion and training for the many eventualities that come with the territory. For me it was pretty much a case of 'get in there, do your best and sink or swim'. I found it to be a sometimes lonely and confronting journey. It takes time to learn those skills and if you do not adapt quickly enough you can easily be spat out of the system. I think that is why I have seen so many players come and go, a scrapheap of talented cricketers who might have had a fruitful career had they been more aware and better prepared for the job than simply knowing how to play a good back defence or cover drive.

There are people right across the cricket sphere, playing for schools, clubs, first-class sides and even for Australia, who, I believe, could benefit from having a written introduction or reference point to the many challenges they may face in an elite environment. Coaches, managers and parents can gain a better understanding and increase their effectiveness in their respective roles if they are more mindful of the challenges and opportunities that will confront players as they progress through the ranks. Also, I expect that participants in other sports – and even other fields, such as business – will be able to pick out pieces of information from my experiences and observations that could be applied to their world and help them in their pursuits.

TRAINING

Session by session, stage by stage

I was always meticulous about my training. I enjoyed it, saw it as the foundation of success and wanted to do it better than anyone else. Some of my teammates over the years probably thought I was obsessive about it or maybe even crazy. When I look back on some of the things I did, maybe they had a point. I mean how many people do you know who would spend Christmas Day doing a triathlon with a bunch of ultra-fit geriatrics? Or another Christmas Day batting for hours in the nets after somehow convincing his wife to feed the bowling machine? How many youngsters do you think would have the nerve to tell Rod Marsh that his coaching at the Australian Cricket Academy was soft?

They all occurred when I was a budding batsman from suburban Perth, a face in the crowd of kids who dreamed of playing for Australia. They may sound a bit extreme but I was desperate to build my strength, become as fit as possible and do whatever else I could to gain an advantage over the rest. I believed right from the start that results would only come from working harder at training than everybody else.

I was lucky that my dad, Ted, instilled in me and my brother, David, a fine work ethic and basic understanding of exercise and training. Each winter Dad would take guys from our cricket club down to the beach near our house and get us running kilometres on the sand to gain a base of fitness for the upcoming summer. Dad had been a very talented runner in his heyday and was keen to teach us to run with balance and mobility.

After a few weeks of beach running we would graduate to the sandhills, where we ran timed circuits of a path that became known at the club as 'Husseys' Hill'. After that we would train on grass, running 800s, then down to 400s, 200s and ultimately 100-metre sprints. Dad would always monitor our running styles, ensuring we were moving smoothly and efficiently, and all the while building our aerobic capacity and muscle power. We did not really need to do many weights, Dad believed, but when we did use them, they were light because he was adamant that a batsman needed to be proficient in 'accelerating the implement', as he described it. By this Dad meant that it was imperative to have control of the bat at high speed. Therefore weight sessions were always based around moving quickly and assuredly. These routines added up to a great preseason each year. By the time we got to the opening day of each new season we were ready to hit the ground running.

Once I entered the state system at Western Australia my training jumped to another level. Our fitness coach, Neil

Tyndall, introduced me to cross-training, which involved plenty of switching between running and gym circuits. Tyndall – who was known as 'Mad Max' to us players – was a very demanding conditioning coach. I remember finding it hard to stand up after some of his sessions because I was completely exhausted. I absolutely loved it.

At the Australian Cricket Academy training started to become more specific and individualised. Having a personally designed gym program was enjoyable, I found, because it was the first time it was my responsibility to do my training properly. It prompted me to keep a diary in which I would note the number of sessions I was doing, their duration and what I was working on. I would write about how I felt physically and mentally, and whether or not I believed the session was successful. I would even note information like how many balls I faced, what food I was eating and how much sleep I was getting each night. It was around this time, too, that I learned about visualisation, going to grounds before matches to get a feel for the place and looking for any potential distractions or advantages. Which direction will the wind come from? Where will the sun be at different times of day? Where are the short and long boundaries? I wanted as much information as possible. I wanted everything accounted for and I wanted no stone left unturned.

My hunger for hard work and progress was ravenous. About a month into my time at the academy, during one of our weekly one-on-one meetings with the coach, Rod Marsh, I told him I was a bit disappointed with what was going on. I said I thought we would be training harder, training longer, training better, and I let him know that I had trained harder back in WA.

Rod sat there quietly bristling and twisting the ends of his moustache. For the next month he absolutely flogged us. It made me very unpopular with the other squad members. But I loved the increase in intensity and I remember reporting back to Rod at the next meeting, 'That's more like it.'

These were my days of unburdened motivation. I wanted as much work as possible and found it energising rather than exhausting. One Christmas Day, instead of spending time with family and friends, I got wind of an opportunity to join a masters age-group triathlon. It was a chance I could not resist. I joined a bunch of the fittest seventy-year-olds you have ever seen for a swim, cycle and run – and came near last.

There must have been something about Christmas time that drove me to extremes because another year I coerced my ever-patient and supportive wife, Amy, to feed the bowling machine for hours and hours. I just could not put off for another minute refining my defences and glances, working on my pulls, hooks, cuts and whatever else. Surely, I thought, no one else would be training on such a special day, so I must be getting ahead of the competition.

That theme continued right throughout my youth. When our club team had a bye one weekend I decided that instead of going to the movies or the beach I would take on a roundabout suggestion Allan Border had made to us a little earlier, during an Australia A tour of Scotland. The day before a game over there, Allan blew up at us after we had gone easy in the nets. The bowlers had sent down just a couple of overs each and the batsmen had only a quick hit because they claimed they wanted to be fresh for the game. Allan was not impressed at all.

The old-school hard nut growled at us: 'How do you blokes expect to be able to bat all day when you just want to have a few minutes in the nets?' To the bowlers, he said, 'How do you expect to bowl twenty-five overs in a day when you bowl for ten minutes in the nets?' It really got me thinking about what was the best way to be prepared for a day's play.

When I was back home and Wanneroo had a bye I saw a chance to take Allan up on his dare and bat for a whole day. I asked my wonderful old batting coach, Ian Kevan, to come to the nets with me and we mimicked three full sessions of play. We worked for two hours then had forty minutes for lunch. We had a two-hour middle session followed by twenty minutes for tea. Finally, we trained for another two hours to mirror an afternoon session. It was the kind of work that I believe set me on course for the career I was to have.

Once I got into the Australian team training changed again, with maintenance becoming a priority. Because we were playing for something like nine or ten months a year, preseasons became nonexistent. Instead, the focus was about making sure we did not overdo things. It was about helping each individual stay in one piece. Maintenance was personally tailored for each player. For me, for example, after I had my hamstring problems, it was about exercises to strengthen my legs and loosen my hammies.

Training drills in the Australian team were more cricket-specific than anything I had encountered previously. The running was no longer about flogging yourself to build condition. It was aimed at replicating game situations. We would practise running singles, twos and threes, then recovering. Everything had a rhythm of effort, recovery, effort, recovery.

For the bowlers it was similar – run in, go back to your mark – effort then recover.

At all levels of my journey in cricket I was often lucky to come across people and systems that offered the right types of training for the stage I was at. But I also took initiative. I did a lot of thinking, reading and talking to people about what was the best regimen for me to achieve different outcomes at different times. Training is not something that can simply be left in the hands of coaches or parents. It is a critical aspect of the game that plays an indisputable role in an individual's development. It is therefore, ultimately, the responsibility of the athlete. I believe that all cricketers who want to get the best out of themselves must gain a strong understanding of training in general and what works and does not work for them.

Different strokes for different folks

Amid the many interesting training experiences I was privileged to have over the years, one of the most striking lessons I learned was that training cannot be viewed as a one-size-fits-all process. My desire, for a long time, had been to push myself to the edge. Certainly laziness gets you nowhere. But as I looked around at some of the incredibly successful cricketers I came to call my teammates and opponents, it became clear that what works for one person might not work for another. Sportspeople, like everyone, have unique requirements and motivational triggers. Everyone is distinct and training must be flexible.

Often we talk about the many undiscovered talented sportspeople there may be around us. How many great cricketers – or tennis players, footballers, gymnasts or swimmers – might be out there who never had an opportunity to discover their potential? It's a fair question. But I have also come to think of it the other way around. How many talented sportspeople have we driven away from sport by being too rigid in our perceptions of training?

To always expect athletes to train to their physical limit, particularly in a game like cricket, I believe, blankets us all as being the same type of personality. It suggests we would all respond similarly to the same prompts and demands. Yet players such as Australian coach Darren Lehmann or the brilliant South African batsman Hashim Amla – and scores of others who went on to have fabulous careers – would not have thrived in the kind of hardcore training environment that suited me. Similarly, I would almost certainly have lost interest if I did not find in cricket an avenue for the kind of physical and mental demands I wanted in my training.

When talking about the importance of personally tailored training we must also acknowledge that athletes' needs change. I went all guns blazing when I was young. But as the years went by my regimen evolved and developed. At, say, age thirty-seven, even though I was still very fit, there was no point going full tilt, as I had in my teens and early twenties, because it would not have guided me to my optimum level of performance. My training had to be better timed and tempered.

I saw the same evolution of approaches to training in the guys around me. Two of the greatest players I was fortunate to call my teammates, Shane Warne and Glenn McGrath, at times later in their respective careers seemed to do so little at team sessions that they may as well have stayed home. Yet what they did was perfect for the stage they were at. They knew their games and personal requirements inside out. All they needed from standard training was to get a reassuring feeling that the ball was coming out of the hand comfortably.

I used to be a great advocate for vigorous training to build strength and condition. I definitely still believe young players should push themselves really hard at times as this is the period when you can build a base of fitness that can last years. But my journey has taught me that, at any age or stage of a career, quality is often preferable to quantity. The best trainers I have seen, such as Michael Clarke and Ricky Ponting, have leaned towards perfection over volume. Rather than push themselves to their physical limits time and again they often would concentrate on ensuring that whatever training drills they did were performed perfectly. By doing so they knew they could replicate those drills at the crucial time, out in the middle with the nation's fortunes resting on their shoulders.

Perfect training does not necessarily mean that everything surrounding the session needs to be perfect. One characteristic that made Ponting so outstanding was his refusal to complain when the facilities were not of a high standard. We are very lucky in Australia to have generally top-class facilities. However, overseas I quite often found nets and other equipment to be in horrendous condition. Instead of throwing his hands up in the air and storming off, as I saw many players do, Ricky would look for whatever advantages he could gain from the situation. He saw opportunities to attend to his routines, ensure his gear was being used to its greatest effect and practise surviving on a tough deck. Ricky set a standard for training in nasty conditions.

He would be first in there, set up his session and work away until he got what he wanted from it.

Ricky's approach inspired many of us to follow his lead. Watching Ricky make the most of every situation made me want to get in the nets and battle away, even if I got hit or looked out of sorts. I felt that if I could get through that kind of a session at training I could get through anything in a match. Others, for instance Matthew Hayden, did not feel their interests would be well served batting on bad practice wickets. Matthew believed he gained more from facing a bowling machine for three hours. Who was anyone to argue? Facing a machine and hitting ball after ball got him into a good frame of mind for the rigours of being out in the middle, facing the fastest opening bowlers in the world. Obviously it worked well for him. Different approaches work for different people.

Overtraining

Matthew Hayden, Ricky Ponting and Michael Clarke were all very experienced players who had a deep understanding of what philosophies and styles of training worked for them. But even superstars get it wrong at times. At the second IPL, in 2009, Matthew had one net session the entire tournament. He was out surfing, sightseeing, doing whatever he wanted, and we hardly ever saw him. But his workload must have been spot-on for him at that time because he creamed the opposition and won the award for most runs in the tournament. He batted unbelievably that year.

The next year, I remember, Matt went down the opposite path. He batted and batted and batted in the nets. In fact, I had never seen someone hit so many balls over so many hours. It must have been especially draining given the brutal Chennai heat. I said to Matt, 'You're killing yourself, mate. What are you doing?' He said he was fine and kept charging on. Even the day before the final he batted for an hour and a half in the nets. The contrast with the previous season could not have been greater – and neither could the results. The big Queenslander struggled for runs all tournament.

Matthew was by no means alone in having made a glaring training error. By the time I got into the Australian team I felt certain I had a strong grasp of what I needed to do to be at my best. But I, too, could get it horribly wrong. One of my biggest errors came leading in to our massive series against South Africa in 2008–09, when the pressure of a contest against one of the superpowers got the better of me.

We had recently returned from India and I felt mentally and physically spent. Coming back from India, you tend to feel like you need weeks off because of the sapping heat, tough cricket and general grind. My tour had been good; I had batted for long periods and was our leading scorer. But I had only one day at home before we all headed to Brisbane for the start of the domestic summer. I knew I was tired but my exhaustion was overridden by the excitement I felt about playing at home. All I wanted to do was be ready for our visitors, and I believed that fierce training was the way to go.

Before facing the Proteas we played New Zealand in a two-Test series. I struggled in the first innings of the first Test, largely because, suffering from fatigue, I found it difficult to adjust from the turning Indian pitches to the fast bouncy strip in

Brisbane. I got a bad decision in the second innings and went for a duck before scoring 70 in the second Test, which we won by an innings. Overall I did fairly well against the Black Caps. But things were about to step up a gear and I did not feel like I was where I wanted to be.

South Africa were challenging us for the number-one world ranking in Tests at the time. We all wanted to be at our best for the three home Tests before travelling over there for a return leg. I felt a burning desire to prove I could conquer them. However, by this stage I was really struggling to keep things together and it quickly became apparent that the harder I tried at training the more damage I was doing to my prospects. It was the perfect case of one step forward, two steps back. In hindsight it all seems so obvious. But in the moment I really felt I could break through some sort of imaginary barrier if I just worked more and more.

In the lead-up to the first Test at my home ground, the WACA in Perth, I batted and batted and batted, just as Matty had at the IPL. Yet I never felt comfortable with my form and got caught in a nasty cycle of trying ever harder. Ricky noticed something was up but I was in such an intense zone that his advice went in one ear and out the other. 'Gee whiz, Huss', Ricky said. 'Make sure you save a few runs for the middle, mate. Don't score all your runs in the nets before the Test starts.' I just said, 'Nah, I'll be right.' But he was 100 per cent right. I was overdoing it. It would have been much more productive to have switched off and recharged my batteries after that hectic tour of India and my mediocre series against New Zealand.

I sometimes think of overtraining like a Venus flytrap. It looks attractive and draws you in but more often than not it leads to disaster. The more worn-out you feel the worse you tend to hit the ball and the more work you believe you need to do. At the end of each session it feels like your head is on fire. Sleeping becomes difficult because your mind bounces around and your body feels uncomfortable. You realise you have a match coming up and anxiety grows as the reality sets in that you are not ready. I remember the night before the start of that South Africa series I attended one of my children's kindergartens for a function and felt like a zombie.

Such poorly balanced preparation was no way to get ready to face Dale Steyn, Makhaya Ntini and Morné Morkel. Sure enough, I had a shocking series. There were a couple of bad decisions, a couple of unlucky dismissals. But, looking back, I was responsible for my fate because I had been too intense, put too much pressure on myself and trained myself into the ground. It was a great lesson for me that despite many years of experience I did not have all the answers. It taught me that it was important to always keep thinking, listening and learning and to train smart rather than just train hard.

We tend to overtrain when we believe we are out of form. But it is important not to confuse form with results. Sometimes even perfect stretches of training may appear to yield little. I can recall numerous periods in my career when everything came together brilliantly in practice and I entered matches with booming confidence. I felt I had worked hard but not too hard, was tired but still energised and was tuned just right. Yet I was left empty-handed. Cricket can be cruel in that way. A great delivery, a bad decision or one poor shot and you have to wait what feels an eternity to get another chance to show how well prepared you actually were. It's the same for bowlers. You may have trained beautifully, put the ball exactly where you wanted all day, beat the bat repeatedly yet finish with no wickets. These are the times you need to be mature and patient, avoid the trap of overcooking yourself and trust that your investment in balanced and clever training will pay off.

My best example of such an experience was in the lead-up to the 2010 Ashes, when I was loaded with the added weight of my place in the national team being under genuine threat. Things amped up in the days leading up to the first Test, when I struggled in a couple of Shield games, opening the door for a pile of media stories about why I should not be picked and that my career was over. The frustrating thing was that I had been training so well during that time and felt right on top of my game.

Taking heed of my mistake in that South Africa series a year or two earlier, I refused to give in to overtraining this time and kept faith that I was on the right track. Things started to turn when in my final Shield innings before the first Test I scored a century, which kept the critics off my back, at least momentarily. I then continued my perfect stretch of training in Brisbane in the week before the Test, after which I felt primed to take on England. Still, it could have all been for nothing – I got an edge to my first ball of the series, which, thankfully, landed just short of second slip. After a few deep breaths, I started to work my way into the innings and felt with each passing delivery that my sound base of training was starting to shine through. I went on to make 195, my highest Test score, and shared a record 307-run sixth-wicket partnership with Brad Haddin. I finished second-highest run-scorer in the series, with 570, including two centuries, at an average of 63.3. The critics stayed quiet.

Taking charge of your own training

Sometimes it all goes wrong, as it did for me leading up to that South Africa series in 2008–09 or for Matthew Hayden at the IPL that year. But one of the things that most impressed me about guys like Hayden, Ponting and others from that great Australian team I joined in 2005 was their eagerness to take responsibility and control of their own training and preparation.

I firmly believe in the power of individual player responsibility, or 'ownership', as I like to call it. The great players understand that generally they know better than anyone else what works for them and what tools they should use within the structure to be able to bring out their best. They use support staff and coaches as a resource during training or to bounce ideas off. But they never use them as a crutch. There is merit in accepting advice from trusted sources. However, especially these days, elite environments are so crowded with support staff that it has become very easy for players to switch off and let others make all the decisions for them.

Personal responsibility might sound obvious. After all, it's your body, your performance and your career so, of course, it is your duty to keep track of your needs and output. But I am concerned that the growing influx of staff around elite teams could widen the scope for players to become more dependent on others than on themselves. My worry is that this could lead to an increasing number of players with little knowledge or control over their health and fitness. It could also leave them lacking in one of the most essential of all sporting skills: the ability to make good decisions under pressure.

Within most top sporting teams there seems an endless line of experts and advisors, each looking to justify their position by being seen to make a difference. There are massage therapists and physiotherapists, dieticians and nutritionists, coaches and assistant coaches, batting, bowling and fielding consultants, performance analysts, strength and conditioning people and a host of others. It's easy to lose yourself in a sea of science and technology.

Often these staff make a positive contribution, as they offer players specialised avenues to reach their potential. Psychologist Sandy Gordon taught me various mental skills, including goal-setting, visualisation and routines. Physiotherapist Alex Kountouris's expertise enabled me to stay on the park day after day and helped me learn a lot about my body. Some of the physical trainers we had, including Stuart Karppinen and Justin Cordy, helped me handle the rigours of cricket and gave me a base of knowledge about their work. I enjoyed having access to highly skilled professionals in their fields. They deserve respect for their hard work, knowledge and commitment. For all that they offer, however, support staff cannot go out in the middle and do the job on the field. The ultimate responsibility for performance lies with the player. And a player will feel best prepared if he has immersed himself in the entire preparation process.

As important as it is to take charge of the groundwork to their game, I have noticed that in a lot of teams today, including the Australian team, the balance has become skewed towards players losing the need to think for themselves. Too often players are told to simply 'Turn up here, do this. Turn up there, do that.' When that pattern is repeated day after day, as it tends to be, especially on tours, you do not really grow as a person or a player. You miss out on the opportunity to gain knowledge that can help put you ahead of the competition.

On any given day in the Australian team you would do your work with the batting coach in the nets and then get moved along to the fielding coach. Back at the hotel the fitness coach would knock on the door to tell you it is time for your recovery, get into the gym, get into an ice bath or see the masseur. Later, the psychologist would want to meet to discuss how you are going emotionally. The dietician would want to talk about your energy levels. It would go on and on and sometimes seem never-ending. Often it became quite onerous and, at some point, it began to defeat its purpose.

Several of my colleagues in the national team felt a growing burden from support staff. The increasing level of professionalism resulted in ever more monitoring and structure in how things operated. At the same time the volume of other duties, such as media, sponsorship commitments and promotional obligations, continued to rise. The dialogue in the team was, 'Well, that's just what the modern game is like.' But I do not think it has to be that way. I think we have reached a point where a re-evaluation needs to take place about the best way to use support staff and what effect relinquishing personal responsibility has on performance.

The power of responsibility

The ability to take control of your training is critical because it shows itself in competitive performance. It's not just about deciding whether you should bowl those extra few deliveries in the nets or whether to have a massage instead of an ice bath after a tough session. It plays out in the heat of the moment, in the thick of the action, when everyone is watching you and your team is relying on you.

I remember a one-day match against England at Lord's in mid-2010 when I could easily have let others make the decisions for me and just kept my head down. But I could see that my batting partner was in some bother at the other end and our team needed a lift. It prompted me to start thinking a little outside the box and take some control of the situation. My response was just enough to shake things up and get the momentum swinging back our way.

We had been defeated in the first three matches of the five-match series, meaning the series was lost. However, after winning game four at The Oval we felt determined to finish the one-day leg on a high. After a dicey start we reached 4–106 in the thirtieth over when Tim Paine was dismissed for 54. Paine's exit brought Shaun Marsh to the crease to join me but pretty soon it became clear he was battling to settle in. The aim then was to consolidate our total, nudge singles, pick up the odd boundary and build a foundation. It was a fairly predictable approach given our score and the number of overs that had passed. However, whereas I was able to rotate the strike quite easily, Shaun seemed unable to knock the ball around and I started to feel as though we were getting bogged down.

This was a time when our team was very consistent about when we took our batting powerplays, those important five-over periods in an innings when you could force the bowling team to put no more than three fielders outside the circle. We always seemed to take the third and final powerplay in the dying few overs of the innings, which was logical and was replicated by most other teams. But, with Shaun and me doing nothing more than treading water, I felt we needed to do something different or the game would get away from us.

At the start of the thirty-ninth over I made the call to take the final powerplay. It was a bit of a light-bulb moment. It just felt right to me. We could not waste any more time struggling on as we were and I thought that by taking initiative with an aggressive and unexpected decision we might force England into a defensive mindset and free Shaun up to play some shots. In short, I thought that in this instance, by deviating from our predictable approach, we could divert the pattern of the game and regain the ascendancy.

It worked a charm. The English were taken by surprise and seemed unsure of what to do next. The pressure came right off us and we started motoring along. It was remarkable to see Shaun relax so quickly. Almost immediately he started teeing off and batting really well. He cracked three sixes and four fours on his way to 59. Together Shaun and I put on 107 runs for the fifth wicket. I was out in the last over for 79 and our team total was a healthy 277. We won the match by 42 runs and left the series with our heads held high.

The willingness to make that game-changing decision, I believe, can be traced right back to my desire to take charge of my training from a young age and right throughout my career. It stemmed from my hunger to take control of my game and not leave my future in the hands of others. I was the one out in the middle at Lord's, I knew I was better placed than anyone to sense the atmosphere and where it was all headed. Sure, I could have asked for a second opinion from the dressing room – and, to be honest, I did get a bit jittery about what the coach and my teammates would say when I got back. But, thankfully, it turned out well and everyone was happy.

A younger or less experienced player would never have felt confident making a decision like I did that day at Lord's. Experience gives you the space to take on a greater level of decision-making. But what I think that example shows is that it is very important to be conscious of what is going on around you, to consider your options and think outside the box. By all means trust support staff. They are experts who have a lot to offer. Additionally, however, ask questions, take the opportunity to learn from their expertise and never simply take for granted that their advice is the best option for you. If you feel there are tools and methods that might better suit you, have the courage to speak up. After all, it's your body, your mind and your career.

The power of responsibility: part II

I made a big call taking the powerplay at an unusual time against England that day. But lower-risk decisions by individuals can turn games, too. For instance, one unforeseen shot by a batsman can scatter the field, put doubt in the opposing captain's mind and throw the bowler off his rhythm. David Warner did exactly that in a T20 match against India in Sydney in 2012.

I enjoyed chatting with David after that night, when he hit an amazing six off Ravi Ashwin. He explained that with Ashwin spinning away from the left-hander and the field well set, he discovered the most inviting gap was more easily reached if he hit right-handed. It was a space around mid-on, or mid-off for a lefty, and he realised he could use Ashwin's spin coming into him. As the bowler reached the final instant of his run-up, Davey changed his stance and smacked the ball in the direction he had marked out. He hit it so well it sailed over mid-on for a 100-metre six.

Spectators could have been forgiven for thinking Warner's shot was just a spur-of-the-moment roll of the dice. But that was not the case at all. My brother, David, was playing in that match and revealed in an interview afterwards that the dynamic opener had worked on batting right-handed at training. This incredible stroke was certainly no fluke. It was a calculated and innovative addition to Warner's already impressive repertoire. Rather than just following the tried and tested way of doing things or waiting to be told what to do, Warner used part of his training time to think about what he could add to his armoury. He devised this shot, worked on it, picked his moment and executed it perfectly.

Warner could probably spend his entire career waiting for experts to make all the decisions for him. But he exemplifies why, in my opinion, it's more important than ever for players to go the other way, learn the ins and outs of training, think about their own unique needs and gain a strong sense of ownership of their game.

This is the beginning of an era in cricket when players will come together at different stages of their training and fitness cycles. Some guys may be coming from a Test series, where they were tuned to five-day cricket, others from a state one-day or Twenty20 competition, where they were in a different gear altogether. Some may have just been playing in a tournament on sticky subcontinental pitches, others on faster, bouncier strips in Australia. And, as has always been the case, some guys will be fit, young and bursting with energy, and others older, more cautious and looking to time their run into a match more precisely. Failing to properly analyse your own requirements and leaving all the decisions to a guy with a laptop or clipboard seems to me a bit risky.

Players like Ponting, McGrath and Warne had a tremendous sense of ownership about their training, which shone through in their overall performances. It is one of the great attributes of the best cricketers of today and, I believe, certainly tomorrow. I am adamant that those who steer away from placing all their faith in others to tell them what to do, and accept a generous portion of personal responsibility in their cricket, will get a break on the pack.

T20: Bucking the trend

Whereas today's elite players, I believe, may be prone to getting mollycoddled, they may also be the beneficiaries of a perfect antidote to the trend. I believe Twenty20 could provide an initiative and obligation for players to reclaim a sense of ownership of their game. The nature of T20 tournaments is that players most often assemble a short time before the competition begins. They are expected to have prepared professionally and turn up in as good a shape as possible. Also, the game itself demands that players think on their feet. Guys like Warner, Aaron Finch, Ben Dunk and Glenn Maxwell have been so refreshing for

Australia because they work on their own games, back their unique talents and regularly come up with breathtaking results.

For some players T20 offers no choice but to take control of every area of their game. Brad Hodge is a stunning example of someone who has worked hard for years to understand his requirements to the point that he knows exactly what he needs in all areas. Hodge – now in his forties – does it pretty much on his own, as he plays T20 only and is not part of a state structure. I asked Brad about how he gets ready for tournaments. He said he would have a couple of good hits in grade cricket in the lead-up weeks and work with Dirk Nannes, our former Sydney Thunder fast bowler, who also would be long retired had he not paid meticulous attention to his training and preparation during his career.

Like Brad, Dirk is very in tune with his requirements. He has to be, given he, too, does not play for a state and has no access to all the associated extras. He gets his own physio if he needs it, his own massage therapist, his own coaches for particular parts of his game if he wants. He decides when and how much to bowl in training. There is no one to tell him what to do and when to do it. It is entirely his responsibility and he thrives on it. Both these guys are reaping the practical benefits of harnessing all their attributes – talent, experience and, crucially, the willingness to think and take control of their training and preparation.

The Thunder experiment

Responsibility and ownership in modern cricket are factors I have thought about a lot in recent years. I was pleased, if a little surprised, to find I had an enthusiastic ally in Paddy Upton, our coach at Sydney Thunder. Leading up to the 2014–15 Big Bash League (BBL) I met with Paddy for a chat that led to an invigorating and maybe even agenda-setting move away from the overloaded system of assistants and the tendency to mollycoddle, back to a philosophy of player self-determination.

Looking to come back from another last placing in the BBL the previous season, our new coach – who had been Gary Kirsten's assistant with the Indian and South African national teams – asked me what kind of support staff I thought we would need and who we might approach to work with us. Then he delivered a big off-cutter. Paddy said there were two ways we could set things up. There was the traditional way, where we would have our head coach, our batting, bowling and fielding coaches and the usual legion of support staff. Or, he said, we could have none. I must admit I was a bit lost for words. It was so counterintuitive to everything I had experienced in elite cricket. 'Ah, OK, Paddy', I said. 'I'll have a think about it.'

After my initial surprise the idea of having no support staff steadily grew on me as it tapped into what I had already sensed could work. Further adding to my keenness, Paddy had done a lot of research into this idea, looking at structures within business. He had tested the theory of ownership and responsibility, compared the benefits and drawbacks, and believed the principles would carry over into cricket.

The more I thought about it the more I felt comfortable with the concept of us players running the show, especially in a fast-paced T20 competition. I gave Paddy my blessing. I told him I was confident in the depth of experience we had in the squad, with the likes of Jacques Kallis, Eoin Morgan and me. I felt that asking all of us players to take ownership of the team would give us an indisputable awareness that we were the ones who had to turn things and break from our history of poor results. We would have to take responsibility for our training, fitness and preparation. We would choose the tactics and methods we used in matches and deal with situations in the middle as they arose. There would be no scapegoats if things went awry, no safety blanket, no excuses. The older players would draw on their experience in every facet of the game, on and off the field, and the younger players, instead of running off to the coach or an assistant to solve their problems, would either have to work them out alone or approach a senior player and get a conversation going.

The idea went even further when we told our general manager, Nick Cummins, that we did not want official selectors. Instead, we would have selection meetings as a team. It was no longer a case of such vital decisions being made by a special few. Now everyone would have an equal and important role to play in the team's fortunes. Paddy said he wanted to be seen by the squad as little more than a facilitator, whose job was to ensure everyone had the resources they needed or wanted. The rest was up to us. We wanted input and involvement from everyone in our group. We wanted all the players to have ownership, to truly *be the Thunder*. It was a very powerful idea.

Responsibility across fields

It is not only cricket in which I believe there is a tendency to mollycoddle. Pick any modern professional sport. AFL players, for instance, often look like robots as they train and take orders. 'You go here. You run there. You deliver here' – these are terms they probably hear over and over as they shuttle between support staff members. I wonder how much these guys get space to actually think about what is going on around them in training and what impact that has on their game performance. I wonder how much extra potential they would unlock if they could toss things around in their minds a bit more rather than just following orders. How many more Robert Harveys would there be? Harvey was a player who would always seem to be running off in the wrong direction only for the ball to just fall into his arms. Off he would go and produce something magical.

As Paddy Upton found through his research, the same mentality has infiltrated many workplaces and companies. These days, maybe because it feels like so much is at stake, the tendency is to play it safe and steady. Companies want to demonstrate a methodical and disciplined approach in order to lure investors and give shareholders a sense of assurance. Workers are often given little incentive to think outside the box and test their potential. Many tend to switch to autopilot when, in fact, taking more control and ownership could well lead to unexpectedly positive outcomes.

Individuality is what makes the world an interesting place and brings out our best. But the kind of flair we saw in David Warner's wonder six, I fear, gets doused by restricted and predictable structures. Rugby, soccer – probably netball, basketball and most other sports – seem now to have extremely systematic training environments. The players they breed are often like machines. There is a lot to be said for that sort of production line. But I wonder if the cost of this approach is the individuality that provides some of the great moments in sport.

FITNESS AND INJURIES

What is cricket fit?

In cricket circles you often hear about players who are not necessarily fit in the traditional sense, yet are very 'cricket fit'. Some of the best players ever to grace the field can be categorised like that. Sachin Tendulkar was one, Jacques Kallis another. They were hardly the kind of fine sculpted specimens you might see pumping iron at the gym for hours or beating the pavement running kilometre after kilometre. But they both had an uncanny ability to bat for entire days, remain unfazed when fielding for sessions in a row and, if a sharp catching chance came their way at 5.40 pm on day four, they would almost always snap it up as though it was the morning of day one.

Two of Australia's greatest players, Shane Warne and Glenn McGrath, fitted into that group. They were among the most cricket-fit players I ever witnessed. Neither could run as fast as

Usain Bolt or as far as Rob de Castella. But each could bowl long spells and remain switched on until the winning runs were hit on the final day.

McGrath was never one to set the pace with his beep test times. He certainly did not have the best running endurance capacity and was no muscle man. Yet he could operate all day and rarely lose his line or length. Sure, his action was very economical. But being able to produce twenty-five or thirty near-faultless overs day after day in Test cricket could not be attributed solely to economy of movement. It required exceptional knowledge, focus and discipline. It required a high level of cricket fitness.

Warney was a great example of what fitness in cricket means to me. You would never see him running up sandhills or grinding away on an exercise bike. But once the ball was in his hands he would click into gear and immerse himself in the contest. He loved it, thrived on it and his energy stores seemed to multiply many times over once it came time to compete. No matter what the conditions or game situation, Warney produced the same high level of output. It was a marvel to witness and, I believe, an essential complement to his brilliant technical skills.

It is not only in cricket that unlikely specimens turn out to be deceptively fit. Counterintuitive concepts of fitness apply across sports. The ability to know when to make that dash down the sideline in a soccer match, step up a gear in a game of tennis or pick the right opponent to try to sidestep in rugby each come down to sport-specific fitness and aptitude levels. Tony Lockett was hardly triathlon material and probably nowhere near the fittest player in Australian Rules football as we might usually perceive the term. But he dominated because of his awareness, concentration, confidence and power. The baseball superstar Barry Bonds was another who did not comply with the common image of the ultra-fit performer. Yet he was able to use his finely tuned sport-specific attributes to dominate his peers.

In cricket I regard a major component of fitness to be the ability to physically and mentally lock yourself into the battle for six hours a day, five days on the trot. It's about making fewer mistakes than your opponents across that time, ultimately aiming to make as few mistakes as humanly possible. It is as draining a requirement as you will find in any sport. Tendulkar, Kallis, Warne and McGrath were each incredibly successful in this aspect of our game, forging great careers out of remarkable mental toughness and exceptional competitive spirit.

Fit for a purpose

Great players demonstrate that fitness is about being primed for a particular purpose, not just attaining a high level of cardio-vascular or muscular strength and condition. It's generated by clever and targeted training. It's no surprise that many of the principles transfer from what we discussed in the previous chapter.

I used to work myself into the ground day after day, believing that good training was all about volume and exertion. I ran up sandhills, pounded the pavement and batted in the nets until I was spent. But as I learned more about high performance and my individual requirements I found that my training needed to be better tailored. There is no use running 100-metre sprints all day when as a batsman I would rarely need to sprint more than the length of a cricket pitch at any one time. It's about training for the moment of reckoning, training for a singular purpose.

On that basis, a measure of fitness should be the degree to which you can perform in the toughest moments you will be confronted with. It could be at any stage of the day or match. You will call on your fitness when you are starting your innings and the fielders are crowded around you, sledging and niggling, looking for any sign of weakness. You will call on it when the opposition is 3–300, you have 0–80, it is 5 pm, thirty-five degrees, and your team needs you to charge in. You will call on it when you have been standing at slip all day, the batsmen have not edged one in hours but suddenly a nick comes flying your way and you are expected to hold it. To execute in these moments you need a focus and sharpness that goes beyond just being able to run far or lift heavy weights.

I found there to be no tougher examination of my cricket fitness than playing in India. Whereas the Queenslanders, such as Matthew Hayden, tended to be mostly unaffected by the sapping humidity, I really struggled. I felt like I was cooking from the inside. By contrast, Hayden hated the desert-like heat of Perth and battled with dryness in his eyes and mouth, while I felt much more comfortable in those conditions.

I admit there were times when the Indian environment got the better of me. It felt almost like a relief to get out sometimes because I knew I could head to the dressing room and plonk myself in an ice bath. Then I would sit there and think, 'Wow, I really threw that innings away.' I would wish I had stayed tough for another ten minutes, seen off a bowler's spell or got through to tea. I would feel intense disappointment that I had surrendered to myself. I would wish I had been that little bit more resilient. I would wish I had been that little bit more cricket fit.

I played so much in India that later in my career I could almost pinpoint the moments when dangerous thoughts would enter my mind. Toxic statements would infiltrate my thinking. 'I'm just going to slog this one over here' or 'I'm going to knock a single now because it's too hot and I don't want to push the twos'. These were obviously poor decisions but fatigue would be so cutting and so intense that I would feel powerless to deny it.

As time went on I came to better understand how fitness for a particular purpose could be applied in such moments. It made me want to work on my mind as much as my body and, in a way, apply my physical fitness towards making good decisions under duress. It led me to create a fitter state of mind, which enabled me to better stay in the moment, stay focused and win the mental battle. These were the kinds of small advantages that could make the difference between success and failure in our challenging game.

With more experience and knowledge came an increased ability to stay on top of my physical fitness, which provided me with higher confidence, a launching pad from where I felt capable of taking on anyone and any situation. I knew I could bat all day if needed, even in the most oppressive conditions India could dish up. I knew I could concentrate on every single delivery hours into my innings or in the field. I knew my fitness gave me the sharpness and endurance required of a top cricketer, the ability to seize those little opportunities that could turn matches Australia's way.

Dealing with injury

Understanding the way the mind plays tricks in different situations is a key to overcoming our game's fitness obstacles. But it is not only on the field that challenges arise. Part of being an outstanding player is having the ability to apply knowledge and discipline to unforeseen challenges, such as injuries.

The two biggest injuries I had in my career were hamstring tears. It is ironic because I had always worked particularly hard to build leg strength as I considered it necessary for the explosive power needed in batting and fielding. I thought that having good leg strength would help me avoid some of cricket's most common injuries. Paying special attention to my glutes, calves, quads and hammies became a major focus of my training. But nothing can ever be taken for granted when you are exerting yourself for long periods in our demanding game.

My hamstring tears were quite different, presenting contrasting requirements for my physical rehabilitation. One was quite straightforward, the other much more serious. Each injury tested my cricket fitness in different ways mentally, too, occurring amid distinct settings. In one case I had time and space, in the other I felt pressure and anguish.

The first injury happened during the semifinal of the T20 World Cup in South Africa in 2007 in quite bizarre circumstances. There was no warning sign, no tightness in my legs, I had been playing well and felt in a good frame of mind. I took a regulation single, turned for a quick second and slid my bat in to make my ground. In that final instant it felt like a snake jumped up and bit me on the back of my left leg.

I had never injured a hamstring before so I had no idea how serious the problem was or even how a hamstring tear was supposed to feel. I hobbled around the crease a bit, hoping the pain would go away, but it became obvious there was an issue. Our physio, Alex Kountouris, came out onto the field to assess me and suggested I retire to get some treatment. I did not want to hear that and was adamant I could run off the twinge and get on with my innings. I thought that by leaving the ground I would be taking the soft option and letting the team down.

I got it wrong. I could not move well enough to get into good positions to play shots. Fighting on risked making the injury worse and leaving my team short down the track. Not surprisingly my decision to press ahead did not go down well with Ricky, who was not interested in having a batsman who was unable to run quick singles in the middle on such an important occasion. I guess the six I hit the very next ball made Ricky a little less uptight. However, the captain was right once again and the best thing to do – for myself and the team – was to leave the ground and get medical attention.

Back in the change room Alex got an icepack strapped to the back of my leg. Until we could get a scan done there was no way of telling the extent of the injury. But he knew that a lack of leg strength almost certainly equated to a hamstring tear. Over the next eighteen hours Alex wanted me to apply ice for twenty minutes on and one hour off, including overnight. My alarm was set for every hour and I made sure I did what Alex told me. He was great about it, too, coming into my room each hour to make sure I was following the plan.

The next morning I was exhausted. But the thing that sticks in my mind was just how incredibly painful my leg felt. It was so sore I had to ask Alex to put my shoes on because I could not even bend down. That is when the penny started to drop that I was in real trouble. The team was heading to India for a one-day series soon after the World T20 but there seemed little chance that I was going to join them.

Scans showed the injury to be a common hamstring tear. As unexpected and unpleasant as it was, it held few surprises in terms of what I had to do to get back to playing. My role in making a quick and full recovery was to stay disciplined, methodical and stick to the advice I received from the West Australian medical team.

I had a couple of important circumstances work my way. I had the advantage of a clear marker on the calendar to aim for: the first Test of the Australian summer against Sri Lanka in Brisbane, which was well beyond the projected recovery time, reducing the potential for an anxious race against the clock. Also, there were no Tests scheduled before Sri Lanka's visit, alleviating whatever concerns I may have had about another player stepping in and snatching my spot in the side. While the team headed to the subcontinent for the one-day series I headed for Perth, pleased as I could be about a situation that minimised the potential for confusion and stress.

After an initial short period of rest I began doing leg curls to strengthen the hamstring. Soon I was running again, gradually increasing my speed and duration. Eventually I was able to do light batting sessions and some fielding, building up the amount of activity with each passing day. Things moved along quickly and I even managed to get a Sheffield Shield game and one-dayer for WA in before the first Test, which gave me peace of mind before taking on the Sri Lankans.

In some ways I could even argue that the injury was fortuitous. My leg felt strong again and, whereas most of the other guys came back from the India tour exhausted, I felt fully restored and bursting with energy after a long break and gradual build-up. That freshness showed in my performances as I scored a century in each of the Tests, helping Australia to a 2–0 series win.

I felt pretty good about the way I had handled that injury. I had been relaxed and orderly and followed the program set for me to the letter. It allowed me to get back onto the field in great shape. If only all stints in rehabilitation were as simple and straightforward ...

Four years later, in a match at the MCG, Shane Watson compiled one of the great limited-overs innings by an Australian when he scored 161 not out, leading us to mow down England's 294 for a memorable six-wicket win. For me, though, that night became more notorious than memorable as I again injured my hamstring. On this occasion the timing was terrible. It was just a month out from the 2011 World Cup and it began one of the most physically and emotionally gruelling stretches of my career.

The initial turn of events was almost exactly the same as in the first hamstring tear. While going for a second run I felt a lightning bolt go up my leg. However, there was a major difference. This time when I stretched out immediately afterwards I felt no pain whatsoever. There was a slight feeling of weakness like last time but no real inhibition. I felt certain I could bat on. After I was dismissed and returned to the dressing room a fairly regulation decision was made by our medical staff to do a proper check to be sure there was no hidden damage. The next morning I went with Alex and Trefor James, our team doctor, to have a scan.

I was completely confident my little leg niggle would be no problem at all. But I could not have been more wrong. Shortly after the scan Alex and Trefor walked into the room with long faces. 'I hate to say it, Huss, but it's probably the worst possible news' – I cannot forget those words. That little lightning bolt I had felt was in fact my hamstring rupturing where the tendon joins the knee. The reason there was so little pain, they explained, was that it was a complete tear. Had it come only half off I would have been in terrible bother. But a complete rupture, like a complete ACL rupture, becomes painless shortly after the initial sting, belying the severity of the injury.

This time there was to be no relaxing recuperation. I required an operation in which the surgeons grabbed the hamstring, stretched it back down like an elastic band and reattached it to the knee. It was painful and deflating and left me staring down the barrel of a twelve-week recovery. And, the medicos said, that was being optimistic.

Simple arithmetic told me that even in the best-case scenario the next time I would be available for Australia would be for the second or third match of the World Cup. It was a setback, all right, but I refused to be daunted. Immediately I switched all my thinking towards being back in the action and joining our campaign. What I did not see coming was a battle that had nothing to do with what the doctors had laid down.

Our coach, Tim Nielsen, and the national selection panel, for some reason, decided on a policy that each player had to be 100 per cent fit for the first practice match before the tournament in order to be considered for selection in the World Cup squad. I was stunned by this sudden announcement. It had come out of nowhere. It felt to me an unreasonable, poorly considered and unnecessary policy. I began arguing my case.

I told the brains trust that World Cups were not won in practice matches or even in the group stages. They were won by building momentum and playing your best cricket towards the back end of the tournament. As a precedent, I cited the case of Andrew Symonds. At the previous World Cup Andrew had come into the team after the third match and performed strongly, especially late in the tournament, having earlier ruptured his biceps muscle. It felt to me an open-and-shut case, and I was hell-bent on getting them to change their tune. But they would have none of it. When the final call came from chairman of selectors Andrew Hilditch to say their position was final and I was out, I was overcome with disappointment, to say the least.

My focus on recovering quickly took on a new edge. Far from being resigned to the situation and calmly following orders, as I had with my first hamstring injury, this time I was driven by a significant added motivation to put egg on the faces of the national selectors. Back in WA, I pushed my rehab hard, determined to get back to Shield cricket inside twelve weeks and score big runs so I could show them what they would be missing at the World Cup. After my initial recuperation from the operation my recovery started moving along much quicker than even the most optimistic prognosis.

I was in a real hurry and told WA coach Mickey Arthur I was ready to play in a Shield game against Tasmania starting on 21 February, the same day as Australia's opening match of the World Cup, against Zimbabwe in Ahmedabad. But Cricket Australia (CA) overruled my wishes, only fuelling the fire inside me. They could not stop me playing the next game and I made my return in WA's match against Queensland in Perth in the first week of March. I scored only 30 runs in my two innings in that match but it was enough to prove I was up to the task of playing again.

A few days earlier, as sometimes happens on tours, a spot in the squad opened up due to injury when it was decided Doug Bollinger should return home for surgery on his troublesome ankle. Australia's batting had been a bit brittle in the opening clashes and there was now an option for the selectors to replace the left-arm paceman with a left-handed batsman, a considerable asset on the turning subcontinent pitches and one that our squad was lacking. At the end of the Shield match, Hilditch called and asked me to join the team. I hopped on a plane to India, slotted straight in for our match against Kenya and scored a half-century in our 60-run win.

Sadly our team did not progress much further in the tournament. We were beaten in the quarterfinal by India, meaning there was to be no fairytale finish to my comeback and no fourth consecutive World Cup win for Australia. However, on a personal level I felt vindicated in my earlier stoush with the selectors over their squad selection criteria. It had felt hugely satisfying to have overcome such a serious obstacle so rapidly and be able to join the Australian team again for such an important tournament. Nevertheless, there was a niggling feeling in me that the way I had, to some extent, let emotion overtake reason in my recovery had been the wrong way to go.

Those were high-intensity days with little space to reflect. But with the passing of time the lessons those injuries taught me became clearer. The physical foundation of my recovery each time was to execute my rehabilitation programs diligently and without cutting corners. But several psychological factors had arisen that needed to be addressed just as smartly, as they had a direct impact on that physical foundation. These factors tapped into the kind of mental aptitude that I regard as an important part of cricket fitness, the kind of attributes that enable some players to restore and get on with their careers after injuries while others risk falling off the pace.

Nearly all players who go through a period of rehab will tell you it is a struggle to stave off negative thoughts. I had many worst-case scenarios enter my mind, especially the second time, which led me down the path of making poor decisions, in much the same way as I had made poor decisions batting in the Indian heat. I had felt forgotten by my teammates, who pushed ahead with their careers without me. I was anxious that someone would pinch my position in the team and hold on to it and was resentful at being powerless to stop it happening. I rushed my return, driven largely by the anger I held towards the selectors, without reasonably assessing the potential for a re-injury that could have jeopardised my career.

Other thoughts had messed with my mind. Will I be the same player when I return to the field? Will I be able to bat as well as I did before? Will my reaction times be as swift? Will I have the stamina I once had? Will my teammates want me back? With each injury I had gone from being right in the middle of the action, travelling around, training hard and playing at the top level, to suddenly being stopped in my tracks and left isolated, worried and dealing with a very different reality. These were great tests of my fitness to be an elite cricketer.

The great workload debate

If any players in our game need to be well equipped to deal with injury, it's young fast bowlers. In recent years especially it is remarkable to think how regularly the best up-and-coming pacemen in the land have had their progress stopped by breakdowns. We have a very exciting array of quicks coming through at the moment with the likes of Pat Cummins, Josh Hazlewood, Mitchell Starc and James Pattinson likely to spearhead our attack well into the future. Yet so many of the young brigade have had to recover from major setbacks and work their way back.

To some extent we should not be surprised. Fast bowlers have always been the workhorses of our game and susceptible to breaking down. The physical demands of bowling seem pretty much destined to cause problems. The whipping action and repetitive transfer of weight place tremendous pressure on the body. Even bowlers with beautiful, smooth styles encounter problems. Brett Lee had a textbook fast bowler's run-up, stride and delivery but he, too, spent considerable time out of the game nursing back and ankle issues.

The likelihood of injury from fast bowling is high. But age does play a role. From my observations of playing with and watching guys like Bruce Reid, Brendon Julian and Tom Moody, bowlers tend to have a golden run of fitness between twenty-five and thirty, when their bones and muscles are strong and they stay in the game for long stretches. But between the ages of eighteen and about twenty-three they nearly always spend some time on the sideline, generally due to some sort of back strain. The body at that time in your life is simply not developed to the point where it can withstand the rigours of bowling day after day.

Plenty of research has been undertaken to try to reduce the incidence of injury, especially among young fast bowlers. So much volume and variety of cricket has been packed into the schedule in recent years that sticking to structured workloads has become an essential part of bowlers' programs. Yet it is a very touchy subject. For as long as workloads and rotations have been part of the modern game there has been conjecture. A lot of it has been quite heated. Almost everyone seems to have an opinion, not least the bowlers themselves, who seem split on the idea of rest and recuperation versus maintaining a high and consistent level of output.

The key is that, like training regimens, one policy cannot work for all players. It is one reason why I have tended to sit on the fence when debate has raged about whether this player or that player should sit out the next match. I know there are advantages to getting a large volume of work under your belt when you are young. I got a large volume under my belt as a youngster and it helped me. But I also know that a lot of time, effort and expertise have gone into the science that shows that bowlers, especially, need breaks to allow their bodies to recuperate.

Points of conflict are inevitable. Players are different emotionally, not only physically. Who is right when, say, Mitchell Starc is told to bowl no more than eighteen balls in a net session but he believes he would feel better prepared for the next match by bowling half-a-dozen overs? Who should have the final say, the scientist or the bowler? Even when analysis and statistics showed I would be best served being rotated from the side, I was never happy to be told to have a rest. I had spent ten years trying to get just one game for Australia. I did not want to have a rest. I did not want to sit by while another player was given the chance to impress. The thought of taking a break made me feel anxious and upset. It suggests that in some people the physical advantages of being rotated might be outweighed by the negative mental cost.

It took a lot of experience and patience to finally come to accept that the packed calendar would inevitably take a toll, fatigue would kick in and my body would start to taper off. It was better to take a scheduled break than face deteriorating performances. My fears and anxieties had to be tempered by the understanding that I was doing the right thing for myself and my team in the long run.

The concept of managing workloads has been hard to teach players let alone explain to the public. It has been made harder by former players lining up to criticise the policy. 'Ah, he should just get out there and bowl and bowl and bowl', some would say. 'Back in my day we just got on with it. We didn't need rests.' But it is very naive for those old blokes to say such things without being able to back it up with any data or research.

My experience of playing the modern game, as well as reading publications such as the 2013 Australian Cricketers' Association State of the Game Report, has left me in no doubt that the 'back in my day' attitude is no longer viable. Highly educated and professional sports scientists studying this issue, I would suggest, know much more about fitness, physiology and injury prevention than old ex-cricketers. The game is completely different now. Monitoring of workloads and taking scheduled breaks has never been more important. Our young fast bowlers are very much at the coalface and the more research undertaken to help them avoid injuries the better.

Workload hypocrisy

While there is some validity to the argument that players are best placed to determine their workloads, I think we have seen in recent years that even those very personal judgements can be clouded by external factors. Where once players were adamant they were being forced to play too much, most are now lining up to play more and more.

As an executive member of the Australian Cricketers' Association I participated in a lot of ACA meetings around the middle of the last decade where we discussed players' grievances about scheduling. One argument was that there was too much cricket without context and a risk the public might lose interest. Another argument was that the demands on players were becoming too great. There were complaints of fatigue and stress from being away from families for long periods in a seemingly relentless drive to play more and more. Ricky Ponting was vocal about it, as was Tim May, who was the head of the ACA and, later, the Federation of International Cricketers' Associations (FICA).

Then a strange thing happened. Almost immediately after the IPL was established in 2008 the debate seemed to vanish. The IPL – which gave players the chance to make unprecedented earnings for a few weeks' work – was scheduled around April and May, generally a small window of time each year when Australia's national representatives and fringe players could return home, switch off from cricket for a while and be with their families. Now few seem bothered about the packed itinerary. On the contrary, most keenly added this new component to the season, an intense period of playing and travelling – in India, no less. Frankly there was no escaping the fact that players were choosing the money over continuing to pursue a better balanced program and better assistance in helping them stay fit, fresh and injury free.

At the time of those ACA discussions my viewpoint was that there was not too much cricket being played. However, I was a relative novice at the time, still fresh in the Australian team, and I remember Matthew Hayden cutting me down. 'Mate, I'll ask you about workload in a few years' time', he would say. And he was right. As the years passed, I came to understand just how hard it was to stay fit amid relentless playing, travelling and performance pressure.

The emergence of the third brand of the game, Twenty20, made reconsidering the programming of cricket even more urgent. But the players' keenness to be involved meant our tactic had to change. Instead of looking to reduce the amount of cricket played, we attempted to negotiate better gaps between games in order to give players time to recover. Yet that argument, too, fell mostly on deaf ears. The money-making machine was in full swing and nothing was going to stop it.

I think both parties – the players and governing bodies – have been guilty of self-interest throughout this entire discussion.

From my vantage point I could see how they fed into each other, making the debate about scheduling, protection of players' health and the strength of the game a complicated web.

The boards were never going to actively pursue a reduction in the amount of cricket being played because every game meant more money in the coffers. Their interest was, is and will likely always be primarily in the bottom line. From the point of view of the players, even though we had always been paid well by Cricket Australia, we had also seen the ruthlessness the selectors had shown in abruptly ending the careers of many of our teammates. We felt that if the selectors believed a player was done they would discard him without hesitation and move on. We saw what had happened to Mark Waugh, Ian Healy and Michael Bevan. It created a sense within all of us that we needed to be more vigilant about looking after our own backyards. The IPL provided the perfect answer to those concerns.

For guys on the periphery the IPL was a fantastic option. All of us could understand why, say, Brad Hodge would be willing to push his fitness to the limit and risk further international selection to play T20. Hodge had worked extremely hard to play for Australia but was rewarded with just six Test appearances. His international career seemed to constantly hang by a thread. How could anyone begrudge him playing in India, where he could make good money and secure his future?

The emergence of T20 empowered players financially but added a whole new dimension to the fitness challenge. Calls from CA, the ACA and even top players to self-monitor workloads, show restraint and concentrate on recovery and recuperation were drowned out. It is a reality that remains today and appears unlikely to change.

Eating, sleeping and taking supplements

At the IPL and other T20 competitions the testing schedule means meal replacements and nutritional supplements are probably necessary. Being part of a T20 competition might look glamorous but all that glitters is not gold. There are big challenges in overcoming unusual sleeping and eating patterns. There is constant travel, which gives you the feeling of being permanently jet-lagged. There is a never-ending flux between the emotional highs of match days and the boring and claustrophobic lows of being stuck in a hotel for long periods.

On IPL time it is rare to get back to the hotel before midnight. You might find yourself in the middle of a tense match at 11 pm. Unstructured eating times complicate the situation. On game days it is rare to have more than just lunch and a light supper before the match. Across the afternoon and evening medical staff provide you with meal supplements to keep your energy levels high. It is a precarious balance, putting your trust in someone and hoping they give you what you need to stay healthy and fit and to fuel your performance in trying and unusual circumstances.

There are few regular patterns in T20, let alone for mealtimes, perhaps opening some leeway for the supplements to fill in gaps. Yet in everyday life in the Australian team I found the approach to be very similar. A lot of money was spent on the latest and best supplements, a large emphasis was placed on their use and players were strongly encouraged to take them.

My memory of being in the Australian team was that at the end of a day's play you would return to the dressing room and on your chair would be a cup filled with fish oil, multivitamins, glucose products, protein, creatine and who knows what else. I would throw the contents of my cup down my throat and never think twice. I was in essence entrusting my entire career – everything I had worked for – to a handful of support staff who picked and chose what I would put into my body. In hindsight I feel it was a foolish thing to do.

I am not suggesting any players or staff in the team did anything outside the rules. We certainly never received injections. Injecting substances would have been the point at which alarm bells would have gone off, in my mind at least. However, my experience with being part of a supplement regime in an elite sporting environment has led me to feel some sympathy for the players at Essendon and Cronulla. They got into trouble for pretty much doing exactly what we did. The footballers at those clubs would have had people telling them that what they were doing was right and all above board. Only later did they find out that was not quite the case. I can only imagine if that had happened to me. It would have been an enormous shock and deeply upsetting.

We, like the footballers, were told year after year in drug agency meetings and lectures that what went into our bodies was ultimately our own responsibility. We would have to bear the consequences for any transgressions, including potentially career-ending bans. Yet we never put those warnings to great practice. At the end of each day's play you would come off the field buzzing with a mixture of exhaustion and adrenaline.

The fitness staff you knew and trusted would hand you your cup of supplements and that was that. It's crazy when I think about it now.

I have not been in an Australian dressing room since 2013 but I hope that in the wake of the supplements scandals in the football codes things have changed. I hope players are asking questions and learning more about what they are being given. I hope it has opened the door for more discussion about diet and nutrition overall as a fitness tool.

Whereas supplements were very much in vogue, in my experience in the national set-up there was hardly any discussion about diet. We were not educated about it, and I never knew what to eat and how to get the most benefit from my food intake. Perhaps if there was more attention paid to nutrition there would have been less need for supplements.

A diet of success

The Australian team's playing environment may not have encouraged much interest in diet but the best cricketers take it upon themselves to learn about how nutrition can work for them. They create their own rules and regimens around what they put into their bodies. Peter Siddle was a great example, not only showing that change is worth embracing if it is well thought out, but also demonstrating the power of diet on physical and mental health and fitness.

It was a remarkable transformation for a bloke who was well known for playing just as hard off the field as on it. Peter loved his cricket and trained well. But he also ate a lot of rubbish, drank alcohol and loved to party. After a Test match it was well known that he would have a massive blowout and take his celebrations to an extra level. Sometimes he would binge for days before settling back down into his training pattern. During his early days in the Australian team he got away with it. But, eventually, things came to a head. Shortly after a Test match in Adelaide that he celebrated a little too hard, Peter was hauled before the team and our management and told in no uncertain terms that his behaviour would no longer be tolerated.

The fast bowler from Victoria could have gone either of two ways after that. He could have refused to change and possibly never played for Australia again. Or he could have reassessed his way of life, changed his views and come back a better, fitter and more balanced cricketer. Thankfully and courageously he went for the latter.

It was like a light-bulb moment. Peter realised that his drinking binges had a negative effect on the team and on his cricket, as they lowered his fitness and projected poor discipline. Alcohol was a constant factor in his problems and cutting it out would more than likely help him get back on the right path.

Peter declared to us after that Adelaide incident that he was going to give up alcohol. We all thought, 'Yeah, right. How are you ever going to do that?' But he stuck to it, showing great will and restraint. Test matches would be won, drinks would be passed around and the party would begin, but he would say 'No, thanks.' He was like a new man. That was in mid-2012 and I don't think he has touched a drop since.

A few months later, in November that year, Peter took his new lifestyle another step. He had been in a relationship with a partner who was a vegan, and she began talking to him about the benefits of her diet. He decided to join her and has since spoken about how much more energy he has, how much quicker his recovery times are and how much happier he feels. The one-time party boy's strong decisions about diet, health and fitness have worked wonders and I tip my hat to him.

Peter cops a bit of a ribbing from the boys at times, who urge him to 'Come on, have a steak! Have a beer!' But he has done what he knows is right for his cricket and his overall health and he wants to stick to it. I don't think you can criticise a man who has decided to make a positive change to his lifestyle to give himself the best chance at lengthening his career and, indeed, his life. In future I expect there to be more examples like Peter Siddle, of individuals paying increased attention to diet as part of their fitness plan and making positive and informed decisions in this area.

Meal and energy supplements will probably continue to play a useful role in the T20 environment, where timing and travel make it impossible to stick to a consistent healthy diet. But I think there is a growing awareness of the importance of education and provision of high-quality nutrition within team surroundings. These days you have the Indian team travelling with private chefs and the English team requesting superfoods and hosts receiving extravagant cuisine guidelines. It makes for funny headlines in newspapers, but it's about giving the players every possible opportunity to play at their best.

The trouble with ageing

We have seen how fitness at all levels of the game refers to both physical and mental aptitude. It's about endurance and focus in all conditions, training for a particular purpose and making good decisions whatever the situation. It's about managing your diet and schedule and recovering from injuries in the most effective way. And it's about doing all of these things as well as you can until the day you retire.

I think there is no basis to the claim that players suddenly lose their skills or slow down once they hit a certain age. But there is definitely an added mental pressure that comes from the way the fitness abilities of older players are perceived by others. Talk among teammates, the public or in the media can put demons in the minds of even the most experienced players and prove a major stumbling block.

My belief is that if you start to think you are getting slower – if you think your footwork is not what it used to be or you are not picking the deliveries as well as you did – then those things will happen. I am hesitant to say it but I think that is what happened with Ricky Ponting in the late part of his career. I remember him getting stung on the arm by Kemar Roach at the WACA and it sparking a frenzy of chatter about whether his reactions were slowing down. He had been one of the best players of the short ball in the history of the game and suddenly people were questioning his ability to hook and pull.

I do not think there was any deterioration in Ricky's abilities. I don't think his eyes were going or his feet were moving any slower. But maybe a tiny bit of doubt started to wreak havoc. Maybe all the talk started to fester in his mind and it became a self-fulfilling prophecy. Certainly after that incident he was not as consistent or dominant as he had been for years beforehand.

Ricky never sought to eliminate the hook shot from his game. I'm glad he did not go down that path. I could never fathom how players could suddenly erase a certain shot from their repertoire, as batting is such an instinctive process. But it does work for some and can be a legitimate tactic as a means of negating the mind game that comes with ageing. Steve Waugh famously stopped playing the hook and pull and it worked for him. Sachin Tendulkar was another great who modified his strokeplay as he got older, prolonging his career. Bowlers, too, make adjustments. There have been numerous examples of fast bowlers who have gone from bowling flat out to concentrating more on swing and cut as they have aged. At some point, some players with longevity will make subtle changes to their game in order to stay at the same level.

I never felt that my reaction times were slowing or that I needed to adjust my game in any way as I entered my late thirties. Physically I felt fresh and strong and I felt more than ever that I knew my game and requirements. The one way in which age became a burden for me was when Michael Clarke took over as captain and I started to sense that age could be used as an excuse to drop me.

Michael held very high expectations of players' fitness. He saw it as a key element in our success and wanted everyone to be on the same page. His message became loud and clear: you must be up to scratch with your conditioning or you will be unlikely to be selected.

Rather than eliminate strokes or modify my game, Michael's expectations prompted me to work even harder to be as fit as possible. If I had a bad patch with my batting it would have been very easy for the selectors – of which Michael was one for a while – to say 'He's getting a bit older, his fitness levels are not what they used to be, so we should drop him.' It made me absolutely determined to be in the top five each time there was testing and ensure I performed well in all areas. I did not want to offer any easy excuses to be dropped. Thankfully I managed to take my age out of the equation, at least among the people who mattered.

MENTAL PREPARATION

The moment of truth

One of the big problems with cricket, especially Test cricket, is that there is so much time to think. While you're batting, there is time to think. When you're waiting to bat there can be hours of time to think. If you get out cheaply thoughts pour through your mind. In the field there is so much time to ponder and stew. Strategies are essential to maintaining a positive frame of mind so you can remain stable and concentrate.

I believe, for a batsman, the really critical point for thinking is those few moments spent taking guard at the crease at the very start of an innings. It may seem like a drop in the ocean of a full day's play but a solid and peaceful disposition in those couple of minutes can set the scene for you for hours to come.

The process begins with the walk from the dressing room to the crease. Every player has some degree of apprehension as they walk out to bat. It is almost impossible to completely shut down negative or worrisome thoughts. I can think of so many different doubts and questions that have raced through my mind as I have headed out to the centre. Most often they're about the immediate situation. *What is the pitch doing? How much swing is the bowler getting? How fast is it coming through? Is it seaming around? We cannot afford to lose another wicket.* You think about your own situation. *I haven't scored runs for the past couple of matches. What are the selectors thinking? What is the media saying? Do my teammates still want me in the side? Am I still good enough?* One of the greatest skills I learned was to be able to put those thoughts to one side and ensure they did not impinge on my performance. The key was faith in my lead-up and effective self-talk. It became a fixed routine of mental preparation that worked for me for many years.

On the walk to the crease I would begin the process by reminding myself that I had done the hard work in training. I reaffirmed in my mind that I was fit, ready to compete and belonged in the team. I was prepared for the job I had ahead of me. These truths gave me a sense of confidence from where I could begin the next phase of my routine.

Upon arriving in the middle the intangibles would leave my mind and I would start to follow more practical steps. I would first concentrate on my stance because that is the building block from where everything else grows. Second I would tell myself to relax, let my arms go a bit soft, stop gritting my teeth and let my body go with the flow. The third step was to actively seek to clear my mind of all negativity and doubt.

The way I cleared my mind was to envisage a train pulling up at a station. Rather than let the negative thoughts get off the train and join me I would picture them being taken away, departing the scene as the train left the station. It would leave my mind unburdened. The final step of my mental preparation routine was to focus absolutely every little bit of my concentration on one thing and one thing only – watching the ball come out of the bowler's hand. The end result of this routine was to see the ball large and clear, with a relaxed body and mind. From that point I was able to let my instincts take over.

Simple as it may seem this was a routine that took a long time for me to develop and became one of the foundations of my career from around my mid-twenties. *Stance – relax – clear mind – watch ball.* I went through it every ball at training, throughout matches for Western Australia, county cricket in England and then right throughout my days playing for Australia.

Overcoming mental obstacles

Confident as I was in my set-up routine, and as closely as I stuck to it, external factors always provided variations that had to be accounted for. Low confidence in tough times makes it hard to be in a sound mental-preparation groove. Even when things were going well I found I had to be tuned to the situation. Whereas some batsmen can become complacent as the good times roll, my experience was to go completely the other way and become scared of failure, sometimes to the point where it would become quite debilitating. I just wanted the run to continue. Nerves would build and I would think, 'Please! Just a little bit longer, another month, another week, just another day, please!' I knew that cricket fortunes come in waves and the longer a stretch of good form went the closer the bad times inevitably became.

The longest stretch of good form I enjoyed was at the start of my international career. A lot of it had to do with the circumstances that surrounded me. Not only did everything feel incredibly exciting and new, as it does for all newcomers to the Australian team, but I was fortunate to join a team of highly talented and very successful players.

There was still pressure, of course. I wanted to show that my selection was warranted and I belonged at the top level. I was thirty years old, had been through so much to get there and was determined to do well. Yet I remember playing with very little fear in those early days. If I did not score runs, I knew Ricky Ponting would. Or maybe Adam Gilchrist would. Or Damien Martyn, Matthew Hayden or Justin Langer would. With the likes of Shane Warne, Glenn McGrath, Brett Lee and others to defend our totals, it was a team so full of confidence there was always a feeling going into games that we would win.

With that kind of tension taken away it was a much easier transition for me than it might have been. There were few obstacles to me sticking to my regular mental preparation routine. Everyone was supportive and I just wanted to get out there and play. Without all that much expectation on me, having entered such a successful and confident team, I was able to bat freely and to the best of my ability, leading to a great stretch of personal success. It was a wonderful time.

Bit by bit that feeling of freedom started to tighten. The realisation dawned that with each win or successful personal performance a stretch of poor form loomed larger. People loved asking questions about my average, which stayed high for quite a while, and I would try to steer them in a different direction and soften the inevitable blow for myself by saying it would eventually come down.

When my form began to even out and a gradually increasing weight of expectation started to descend, my efforts to play with mental clarity were significantly impaired. The pressure felt amplified. It seemed to come from everywhere – my teammates, the public, the press and especially from within. Opposition teams were beginning to make things harder as they had more material to work with. They could do more homework on me, analyse my strengths and weaknesses and turn the screws a lot more. Why were the runs not flowing like they used to? It was a question I agonised over at times, leading me to place an ever-growing burden on myself. Conflicting thoughts would enter my mind as I felt that I should, on one hand, play my own way and do what had got me into the Test side in the first place. Yet on the other hand, I started to think I needed to train harder and work out what I could do to get back that feeling of freedom and confidence.

As my consistency decreased a new batch of intense negative thoughts appeared. *Am I going to get dropped? Do my teammates still rate me? Have I been kidding myself all this time?* Media stories appeared with ex-players saying I should be given the chop, that it was my last chance and we should try a newer, younger player. The heat was growing and as much as I tried to filter everything out it became impossible to simply follow my routine of clearing my mind and concentrating on nothing but the ball leaving the bowler's hand.

Amid this maelstrom came a few defining moments that taught me a lot about how I could deal with the obstacles that infiltrated my mental preparation processes. One came during the Ashes in 2009, an unhappy series for our team and for me. On the day of our first innings of the final Test, for some reason the volume on the television in our dressing room was turned up and Ian Chappell was yapping away. 'That's it. Today will be Mike Hussey's final innings in Test cricket', Chappell was saying. 'The Australian selectors cannot persist with this bloke anymore. He's done a good job for Australia but it's time to move on.'

I was a bit upset about Chappell's comments and spoke to Michael Clarke afterwards about it. He said, 'How many times have we seen it, Huss? How many times have we seen blokes in your position come out in the next innings and score a hundred?' I tried to take Pup's rev-up on board but after coming in on a juiced-up pitch following a rain delay I got pinned leg before wicket by Stuart Broad for a duck. I just could not take a trick.

Leading up to my knock in the second innings – having not scored a ton in sixteen Tests – I did a bit of reflecting and put myself in a very different mindset. I remember thinking to myself as I came out to bat, 'Well, if this really is the end – if this is my very last innings in Test match cricket – I am going to make sure I relax, enjoy myself and play the way that feels right to me.' I was determined that my last memory of playing for Australia should not be one of heartache and stress. It should be of pride and enjoyment. 'I am going to play freely', I vowed inside. 'Whatever happens, happens.'

It was much more easily said than done. The reality is much harder when you find yourself in the heat of a fierce battle. But things for me had changed. Not only had I comfortably surpassed my wildest dreams in cricket, I felt a gnawing sense that the game no longer felt enjoyable. At times during that period I had started to question whether I wanted to be in the Australian team. The tension, expectation, negativity and criticism had worn me down. I had put everything into getting there and it had been a great journey. But a big part of me just wanted it to end. With that frame of mind it was a little bit easier to take the pressure off and accept that this could really be my last match on the big stage.

Taking this avenue was not entirely without precedent for me. Back in WA a few years earlier, scratching, kicking and screaming to get into the Australian team, I reached a point where my self-inflicted pressure was so intense that I became miserable and stressed. I decided to allow myself off the hook. I rediscovered my pure love of cricket and suddenly began scoring a mountain of runs. I had felt that whatever the outcome – even if I was dropped from the WA team and never selected again – at least my last memories of playing in that environment would be of enjoyment and happiness. It worked a charm both for my own demeanour and in terms of results, and was a great lesson in mental preparation.

At The Oval that final day of the 2009 Ashes the weight of the world had been on my shoulders. But I refused to feel it. In fact, I felt great. I was doing my favourite thing: going out to bat in a game of cricket. I played positively, like I knew I could, and enjoyed hearing the thud of the ball coming out of the middle of my bat. My feet felt light, my hands loose and my reactions fast. I told myself that this was going to be a great day.

As tends to happen when you enjoy yourself, luck went my way. I was dropped in the slips off an easy chance from Graeme Swann's bowling when I was on about 50. But I felt I was owed a bit of good fortune and I was keen to make the most of it. I continued to play how I wanted to play and ended up scoring 121. When it was all over I was still not sure that my knock would save my career. But I hardly cared. I had batted well, done my best for Australia and scored an Ashes century. Above all I enjoyed myself.

After the series, which we lost so disappointingly, even though the knives had been out, the more I thought about it the more I realised that my performances were not actually all that bad. My average was 35, considerably more than Ricky Ponting and Michael Clarke averaged in the following Ashes in 2011. Combined with the tour games my average was comfortably over 40.

The point is that it was not a train wreck of a tour. Rather, the noise had got to me and made me believe that it was. I *felt* I was on the chopping block. I was being told I was in trouble, my form was shot, my career on the edge and it led me away from my usual routines. I had to battle extremely hard to stay positive and not believe that critics like old mate Ian Chappell were right. Overcoming those negative thoughts and replacing them with positive ones allowed me to play with freedom and enjoy the game again. They led me to score a century that was particularly pleasing.

Buchanan's call

It had been hard for me to break down what was going on in my mind amid all the madness of the Ashes. But there was one man who believed he knew what I was doing wrong and our phone conversation during the series proved another crucial lesson and turning point in my career.

John Buchanan, our former coach, said to me, 'Huss, you look like you're trying to protect everything you've done in the past. You can't afford to play as though your goal is to protect what you've already achieved.' John said I had to keep pushing ahead, back myself to create new boundaries, be positive and relaxed.

John urged me to play as I did when I first came into the Australian team. John saw firsthand how I had gone about handling my first few years in the team and he wanted me to return to that fearless and positive manner. I think John was right on the money. Feeling under siege, my response had been to try to protect what I had done and go into my shell rather than look ahead.

That call from John and the way I dealt with the pressure I felt from pundits like Chappell really changed my perception of how I should play my cricket. I vowed to go out there in a confident and willing frame of mind forever more. I decided to make staying relaxed a priority. I set about enjoying cricket as much as I did when I was a kid and playing my natural game. Whatever happened after that did not really matter. As soon as I made that mental shift I started to play much better. We returned to Australia a beaten team but I felt strong and determined to play my part in the recovery. I scored the first century of the domestic summer and my return to form snowballed from there.

The problem with 'I told you so'

I spoke to Ian Chappell after the 2009 Ashes and he certainly did not back down from his stance that I should have been banished from the team. 'You wanted me gone', I said to Ian. To which he replied, 'Yep. I did.' He's a pretty straight shooter, old Chappelli. Fair enough. He is entitled to express his opinion.

People should be welcomed to express their thoughts about you, your team or any other issue in the game. Cricket belongs to everyone and chatter brings engagement. There will always be people sharing their opinion on who should be selected, who should bowl when or bat where and all manner of issues in the game. The important thing for a player is to recognise that people's beliefs cannot be controlled. What can be controlled is the way we react.

I will admit that after that century in the fifth Test I thought to myself, 'Stick that up ya jumper, Ian Chappell!' I would be lying if I said that I and many other players did not use other people's criticism as extra motivation or, after the fact, a point of added satisfaction. But I know that proving people wrong is not a healthy motivation to use in cricket, whether at Test level or any other level. You should not need fuel from outside to bring out your best. Your drive should always come from within.

It is very easy to find criticism if you want to. Something I have learned since joining the media as a commentator is you can say a dozen complimentary things about a player and one negative thing, and very often all the player hears is the one negative remark. However, if you fall into the trap of using negative comments as motivation you will spend a lot of time filtering through the comments and thoughts of others.

The most obvious way an international cricketer can find negativity is by reading or watching the media. I always chose to avoid the papers and TV commentary if possible because I wanted to try to keep my routines and mental preparation as uncomplicated as possible. I took on board my father's advice that, whatever my form, there was nothing to be gained from reading my own press. He said to me years ago that if a story praised me it could go to my head and I could start believing I was ahead of the game. If a story was negative it was not going to make me feel good about myself or my game. I have kept a lot of articles and asked people to collect them for me. I have a whole filing cabinet full of them and one day I will sit down, go through them and reflect.

Not reading your own press can be empowering in unexpected ways. There have been many mornings at games where I have walked past journalists and said cheerily, 'Good morning, Malcolm! Good morning, Ben!' and they have been very sheepish, trying to avoid eye contact, obviously because they had written something negative about me. They were the ones carrying the uncomfortable feeling. I was happy, none the wiser and focused only on my job of playing good cricket for Australia.

Everyone is different, of course. Marcus North, for instance, used to like reading every single article that was published about him. He wanted to know what was being said, perhaps to use some as motivation, perhaps because he had a bit of a complex about not scoring the runs in Australia that he wanted to.

Marcus scored wonderful hundreds around the world but the Australian public did not see much of him at his best. Maybe he felt the media were unfair to him and needed to be monitored.

Another avid reader was Michael Clarke, who did not let an article with his name in it go by. During my very first Test match, we were driving to the Gabba. Pup was in the front seat of the team minivan, reading a big broadsheet newspaper, and suddenly exploded with a barrage of expletives. He screwed up the newspaper, rolled down the window and threw it out.

All I could think was, 'Why are you doing that to yourself? Why would you read the newspaper on the morning of a Test when it can affect you like that?' No one needs that sort of poison going through their mind when they are about to bat in a Test match. All Michael needed to be thinking about was the next ball he was going to face, not what someone was writing about him in a newspaper.

The best approach for me was to talk to journalists but avoid looking at what they produced, good or bad. I believe you know better than any observer when you are going well or struggling, and you know better than anyone else what to do about it. There are many people who will claim to know what you should do or what others should do with you. But all it becomes is a distraction. Cricket is about minimising distractions, not adding to them.

Staying positive through poor form

Stopping the noise from affecting your performance is hard. Sometimes it's impossible. But confidence is such a flighty emotion that every effort should be directed towards protecting it. Part of this process is learning to draw a line under bad performances and move on. I learned this lesson after a tour of the West Indies in 2008, the first time I really struggled in a Test series.

I had been at the inaugural IPL and came back to an Australian team camp at Coolum Beach in Queensland before heading over for three Tests and some one-dayers. I felt ultra-confident, having had a great start to my career, and keen as mustard to play in a new environment against a good side.

My performances in the three-Test series did not live up to my expectations. It turned out to be one of those cases where anything that could go wrong did go wrong. I would get a jaffa of a ball that would explode out of nowhere or I would play a good shot and someone would take a screamer of a catch. I remember getting out in the last Test match, in Barbados, to a ball from the spinner Sulieman Benn, which jumped off the pitch, took my glove and ballooned out to short leg. I returned to the rooms furiously angry and said something like, 'Well, that just sums up my bloody tour!'

I could see out of the corner of my eye Ricky Ponting giggling, as if to say, 'Welcome to the real world, Huss! Welcome to what Test cricket is really all about.' I took Ricky's unspoken message as a challenge. It was as if he was wondering whether I would pick myself up and get on with the job or throw my hands up in the air and whinge and complain.

Thinking about it that way left me little choice. I had to move on. I had to change my mental reflection on the tour. Instead of feeling hard done by and complaining about it I concluded that I had been a bit unlucky. Things did not go my way, but I could draw a line under it and prepare for next time. I spent time learning from the experience. I looked ahead and felt excited about the prospect of getting back among the runs. In my next Test innings, against India at Bangalore, I scored 146.

This was a process in protecting my confidence, a feeling that can come and go so quickly. It has been fascinating watching teammates and opponents swing from projecting an air of supreme poise and strength to being a frail mess. I remember Clarke often, after getting out cheaply, would honestly believe he would never make a decent score again. He was quite vocal about it too, so you would inevitably try to knock some sense back into him. 'What a load of rubbish, Pup. Of course you'll make runs again', teammates would say.

Shaun Marsh was another player I noticed who struggled to keep an even sense of self-assurance. The selectors had shown amazing faith by picking him as the next cab off the rank to fill Ricky's No.3 position. Yet he had a dreadful series against India in 2011, his first at home, and looked half the batsman he could potentially be. The guys were really supportive of Shaun. They backed him in the press and stood by him privately. Yet with each failure he seemed to become more and more reclusive and quiet.

Shaun looked to me like a ticking time bomb. I spoke to him quite a lot during that period and kept telling him to stay positive. I told him to stick with his game and things would turn. It did not seem to work and he just fell deeper and deeper into a hole. In the end I think he was quite relieved to be dropped. I think it was because he did not know how to regain his confidence and turn things around.

Everyone wanted to help Shaun but sometimes there is nothing anyone can say that will fix the problem. What one person wants to hear another might not. What I was saying to Shaun was probably what I would like to have heard if I were in his situation. But that did not automatically mean it would work for him.

I could relate somewhat to Shaun's experience. During a series in South Africa when I was struggling for runs I turned to Michael Clarke for advice. I asked him if he saw anything obvious that I was doing wrong and what he thought I could do better. His advice was to work harder and harder, keep hitting balls, and things would turn. But it was not what I wanted to hear because I was already hitting ball after ball and working my backside off. What I wanted to hear was what I already knew inside. I wanted to hear him say 'Keep trusting your game. Keep backing yourself. You know how quickly things can turn.' Michael meant well, for sure, but he could not get inside my mind and know what I needed to hear.

In the end I got myself out of that hole and the strategy I used became a helpful way for me to keep on top of my mental preparation. One night I sat down and wrote about each of my dismissals so I could look at them in black and white and think about them. I was able to see that there was a stretch of four or five really unlucky dismissals in my previous ten Tests. There were some bad umpiring decisions, a couple of freakish catches and one or two run-outs that were not my fault. Then I looked at my other dismissals and realised that each one was due to being tentative or in a negative 'just hang in there' frame of mind. There was my answer. I could not change the unlucky dismissals. They will always happen in cricket. But I could change my tentative mindset. I decided to push through my negative feelings and be confident and positive. It was amazing how powerful a decision that was. Suddenly I was moving my feet quickly, swinging through the line of the ball, getting into good positions, moving faster and batting like I knew I could.

Confidence is such a powerful force that it not only works within you but projects outwards and affects people around you. When fielding you can often tell almost immediately if a batsman is in a good frame of mind. Ricky was one batsman who came across as being ready for business and would put the fielding side on the back foot before he had even faced a ball. Matthew Hayden projected certainty and it would really set the tone for his innings. It would send a message to the opposition and, very importantly, it would send a healthy message to all the batsmen waiting to come in afterwards.

Bowlers can gain a lot from exuding confidence. Shane Warne and Glenn McGrath were standouts. I always thought Stuart Clark knew his job well and believed in his ability to execute it. Jason Gillespie rarely gave off a negative vibe. More recently, I was always impressed with the body language of Ryan Harris and Peter Siddle.

Australia's best bowler of recent years, Mitchell Johnson, was a little bit different. I found that he was sometimes less able to maintain a consistent level of projected confidence. Often you would not be able to guess the things Mitchell was thinking about. There might be some off-the-cuff comment that had been made three weeks earlier still going through his mind. There might be a decision made that, because the wind was coming from a particular direction, we should open the bowling with Peter Siddle instead and Mitch would start thinking negatively, worried he was not highly rated anymore. He could be very stubborn about it.

Thankfully, through experience and hard mental work, Mitchell goes about his game with much more stability now. It seems he has got a handle on negative thoughts and is much clearer about his role in the team. At the best of times I did not like facing Mitch. But with that sort of assuredness and confidence he became an even scarier prospect.

Our bowlers' belief in themselves put opposing batsmen off and my recollection is that there were very few who exuded great presence and confidence at the crease against them. AB de Villiers and Hashim Amla were among the more positive performers. Some of the Indian batsmen were completely different at home than they were in Australia. Another who stood out as being very imposing at the crease was New Zealander Brendon McCullum, who appeared to love taking us on. Brendon played some great innings against us because he appeared to us as being mentally well prepared, settled and focused.

Goal-setting

The basis of my mental preparation was to train well, tick all the boxes and leave no stone unturned. But sometimes it is hard to envisage how all those hours of relentless work can translate into scoring centuries or taking wickets for Australia. Setting pie-in-the-sky goals is one thing. But effective goal-setting is something completely different. It's about formulating a plan that has a beginning and an end. It's about mapping out for yourself realistic and attainable objectives that lead you in the direction you want to go. It's the way to give yourself the best possible chance of realising even the most distant achievement.

Most people set goals for themselves, whether it's to get a promotion, make money, go travelling or be a good parent. An eleven-year-old kid might say he wishes he could play cricket for Australia. Any of these outcomes will remain a dream unless there is a well-considered pathway plan. I was taught a four-step goal-setting strategy that worked wonders for me at all stages of my career:

1. **Outcome goal** – This referred to the big, out-of-control end result. For instance, when I was playing Test cricket I wanted to be in the top five players in the world.
2. **Performance goal** – This was where I had to work out what I needed to do to achieve that difficult target of breaking into the top five players in the world. The answer was that I needed to score big hundreds and win man of the match awards. But sometimes those things are out of your control. You might get bad decisions or be run out and not get the results to help your cause. So you have to break it down another level.
3. **Process goal** – This was where I would pose the question 'What do I need to do to score those hundreds and win man of the match awards?' The answer was that I needed to have a very good game plan, play my way, be positive and stick to my routines.
4. **Initial goal** – This was where I asked myself how I would set up those foundations. The answer was to train with

> excellence, complete all my strength and conditioning work, diligently complete my recovery and rehab sessions, write my plans, stick to a good diet and sleep well.

Once you have gone through every step you can see how each level of goal-setting leads to the other. If I work hard at step four, step three will look after itself. Step three will lead to step two. Eventually, if you stay on track and do not allow things to get in your way, step one, the big outcome goal, has every chance of happening.

Meditation

Mental preparation takes all sorts of forms. Different people need different strategies. Justin Langer, for instance, was big on affirmations and quotes. He used to have them stuck around his house to give him inspiration. Other players were superstitious or stuck to particular habits they believed worked for them. Still others used mind exercises such as meditation.

I first came across meditation at the Australian Cricket Academy when I was a teenager and was pretty sceptical about it. To be honest, I could not help thinking it was all a load of rubbish. However, particularly around the mid to latter part of my career, I found it offered real benefits. There is so much stress and pressure in international cricket – as there is in many people's lives – and to be able to escape that for a short while each day became very important for me.

I got right into meditation during a tour of Sri Lanka. It was a period of considerable uncertainty in the team. Tim Nielsen lost his job as coach, Michael Clarke was a new captain and there was a big push for youth to come into the team. I had made one decent score in the one-day series at the start of the tour but had not performed well overall. Out of the blue Clarke said to me, 'Don't worry about not getting any runs in this series, Huss. We still back you and we still see you as part of this team.' Michael's message sent shivers down my spine. Why would he say that to me? Straight away I felt I was on shaky ground.

I had already been through a period of working out how to stay focused and clear of distraction. But this was a particularly difficult time. I needed a new tool to help me set negative thoughts to the side and not let them put me off my game. I decided to revisit the idea of meditating for fifteen minutes a day.

From that point on, wherever I was and whatever was going on around me I would always find a little stretch of time to wind myself down. I would put on some relaxing music, take my mind somewhere other than cricket and find real peace. I would lie down, do breathing exercises and get myself into a positive and calm frame of mind. It was quality, uncluttered time out for myself.

I think it worked because in the three-Test series that followed I was man of the match in each game and won the man of the series. I kept using meditation as part of my mental-preparation routine for the rest of my career and in my life in general.

LIFE IN THE SPOTLIGHT

A bizarre privilege

Life in the spotlight is very much a double-edged sword. On the positive side, each day brings you opportunities and experiences most people could only dream of. Doors open, whether they be to clubs, concerts or events. Meetings with influential or famous people can often be easily organised. Business and sponsorship opportunities land in your lap, enabling you to pick and choose which direction you might like to take them in. It is a privileged and exciting existence and there is much I have experienced through being in the public eye that I am very thankful for.

On the flip side life in the spotlight can sometimes be intense and uncomfortable. People sometimes disregard your personal space and you land in some tricky situations. There are plenty of instances in which well-known people have been targeted by people wanting to make a quick buck or a name for themselves. People make judgements about you from afar, which can be difficult to sit with. Privacy is hard to come by, not only personally but also for your family, including your kids, making it hard to maintain normalcy for your loved ones. It is a story of pros and cons and a predicament for which many cricketers are unprepared.

Throughout my childhood, my early days playing cricket and even up until I became part of the Australian team, being in the public eye was not something that ever crossed my mind. Even when I was watching my idols like Dennis Lillee, Rod Marsh and Allan Border, I never considered them famous or rock star–like celebrities. I just thought of them as Australian cricketers and I wanted to be like them. I had no designs on being famous and had not considered the possibility of being a role model and what that would mean for my life and the lives of the people closest to me.

The blissful ignorance of focusing purely on cricket ended with a thud when, shortly after joining the national team, I went from being a regular Aussie cricket lover to becoming instantly recognisable to millions of people. It seemed surreal. I have so many memories of signing autographs and thinking to myself, 'Gee whiz, why would anyone want me to write my name on a piece of paper for them?' But deep down I could understand it because I had done exactly the same years earlier, running around the boundary chasing Dennis for his signature.

I do not remember any specific incident or moment when it first struck me that I was a famous cricketer. But I do recall that it felt new and exciting and fresh, both on and off the field. It was an amazing experience and I just bubbled along with the flow, trying to take it all in. One of the things that really struck home in those early days was how being part of the Australian team meant that you had the bizarre privilege of being treated like royalty nearly everywhere you went. If we won a match and went to a pub or had a function afterwards everything would be laid on for the team, a section cordoned off and drinks and food brought to us. At the airport there was no lining up like everyone else. You could just zip right through and hop on the plane. We were invited to amazing places, experienced mind-blowing parties and met fabulous people. At virtually any hour of the day or night anything you wanted or needed was provided. It was something I appreciated very much but never truly became used to.

Being a famous cricketer in Australia is weird and wonderful. But it's on a whole different scale in India and some other parts of the subcontinent, where a simple walk to the shops can become a circus. Hundreds of people might follow you. They would look to see what toiletries you're buying, ask for photographs and autographs and just want to chat. It is astonishing to me – even after years of these experiences – that a simple trip to the corner store in India requires a security escort.

Outlandish situations can also arise in other parts of the world. I remember during a break in the Ashes one year one of the boys said, 'Gee, wouldn't it be great to go to the Wimbledon men's final?' Within a few hours we had ten tickets to the final the following day. At the game Adam Gilchrist and Jason Gillespie said they wanted to meet Roger Federer, and again their wish was granted. Incredibly, the greatest tennis player of all met the pair just moments before he was to come out onto centre court. The guys said Roger was so calm and told them he liked cricket, which he had come to know through his South African mother. Then he walked out in front of the world and demolished Andy Roddick in straight sets.

Another truly bizarre memory I have of how ridiculous fame can be was when I told Mick Jagger, 'Sorry, but you're not welcome here.' We were at the 2007 World Cup in the West Indies playing against Sri Lanka in Granada and word came down that the legendary Rolling Stones frontman wanted to visit our dressing room. Ricky Ponting and Gilchrist must have been out in the middle and Matthew Hayden was nowhere to be seen. I was the next most senior player so our manager, Steve Bernard, asked me if it was OK for Mick to come and visit. I said, 'No way, mate. We're playing a World Cup game here. We're still a long way from victory, y'know.' He said no worries and told Mick his request was turned down. Yep, I was the guy responsible for turning Mick Jagger away from the Australian dressing room. As you might have guessed, some of the guys were not too happy with me for that!

Never take it for granted

There are many different ways cricketers deal with the pressure of life in the spotlight. Some players cannot stand it. They go into their shell and wish for all the attention to go away. Others embrace it or thrive on it. My attitude is that being in the spotlight comes with a lot of responsibility – not only to yourself, your family and Australian cricket, but also to the millions of people who love the game and support us players.

In some ways my philosophy is encapsulated in the movie *Pay It Forward.* It was not exactly a masterpiece of cinema but it contained a message that had a big impact on me. It's about a schoolboy who devises a system of doing good deeds for people. When a recipient receives a good deed he or she must do a good deed for three people. They in turn each do a good deed for three further people. And the process continues.

My interpretation of this message is that being kind and thoughtful towards people not only is the right thing to do in everyday life, but also creates a wave of goodness that people notice and remember. When you live in the public spotlight this can become an even more powerful idea because the wave of goodness stretches further and wider than you could ever imagine.

I was brought up by my parents to treat people respectfully and politely. Since becoming a public figure nothing has changed as far as upholding that value. Whomever I come into contact with, whether it is the Queen or a young cricket fan on the street in Mumbai, I try to extend courtesy and respect. Sometimes it has been hard. Cricket can be a stressful environment and keeping a pleasant demeanour can be challenging when the heat is on. There are times you feel angry, frustrated or under pressure and the last thing you want to do is talk to a stranger, sign an autograph or pose for a photo. But it's the right thing to do and I feel strongly that players should be aware of that.

Over a decade or more living in the spotlight I have made a blanket rule of always saying yes to people's requests for an autograph. I always pose for photos or answer questions people might have for me. If I genuinely cannot give people what they would like I will explain politely that I am running late or whatever and apologise. Sometimes in India it is impossible to accommodate everyone because if you do one photo or autograph you will literally have to do a thousand. But the point is that people's support for our game and us as participants should never be taken for granted or thought of as unconditional. Making people feel good about the game and, for me, being known as a good person are as important a legacy as having made a load of centuries.

My determination to act in a respectful manner towards fans of the game has only been strengthened by the disrespectful way I have seen a small number of other players behave. I have witnessed a number of cricketers act in ways that suggest to me they have not properly considered the concept of 'paying it forward'. I have seen players make poor excuses for not paying attention to fans. They act dismissively and arrogantly. 'Nope, I don't sign autographs on Tuesdays', or 'It's past seven o'clock, no more autographs' and they keep walking. If the principle of *Pay It Forward* can work in reverse, the child who waited goodness knows how long for this player's autograph will tell three of his mates that the cricket player was once his favourite but is no longer. His friends will then each tell three of their mates that this player dismissed their friend, and it will snowball from there.

Protecting your family

One of the hardest aspects of being in the public eye, I have found, is ensuring that members of my family can live a normal life. It's one thing for people to want a part of me but it is something very different to think that my wife or kids have to put up with prying eyes or media attention.

Australians are generally respectful of our family's space. But it is always a fine balance. People might yell across the street 'G'day, Huss!' or come up to me to ask how I am going. But there are times when it goes a lot further than that. Going out for dinner can sometimes become deflating because I will have to pose for photographs, sign plates or give the staff something to put up in the restaurant. The dinner is no longer about my loved ones, it's about me and the fans.

Any international cricketer will tell you that after a long tour all you want to do is spend time with your family. I would be on the flight home, daydreaming about taking Amy and the kids to the beach, to a cafe or to the park and making up for some lost time. However, many times we have ended up coming home early or have stayed inside from the start because none of us wants to have strangers coming up to us. We have spent stretches as virtual recluses, trying to keep a sense of normalcy about our lives.

Maintaining a normal life for our kids has always been a priority for Amy and me. We decided years ago that we wanted them to have a strong sense of themselves and ensure they are not thought of as 'Mike Hussey's kids'. It has been challenging. If I help out with fundraising at their schools, for example, I always try to keep it low key. I try to avoid any situation that will lead to them being singled out from the crowds in which they mix. Our aim, like any parent's, is to provide our kids with the freedom to choose any future they desire.

I think most players share my concern for protecting their family's privacy and ensuring they feel supported and loved for their individuality. Not that they often let on. Before a Test match in Perth one summer the former West Coast Eagles AFL coach John Worsfold came to talk to us and I asked him how he protected his daughters from the spotlight and living in their father's shadow. I thought it was a fair and serious question, especially given the goldfish bowl Perth can be. But a bunch of my teammates gave me quite a ribbing. 'Oh, c'mon, Huss! He's not Dr Phil, y'know!' John brushed off the question pretty easily by saying his daughters just get on with life and do their thing. It made me think that perhaps it's easier for girls in this situation than to be the son of a sporting figure.

Another angle on this issue has been my brother's long battle to separate his achievements and history from mine and assert his own identity. He has been sledged plenty of times by fielders calling him 'BOM' – brother of Mike – which really annoys him and is very unfair. David is a highly accomplished cricketer who has achieved great success in his career. I never set out to have him live in my shadow and he definitely does not belong there. He has felt very strongly about making his own way and not being compared to his brother and I always felt he deserved to be treated accordingly.

Image, brands and other uncomfortable terms

In so many areas of life today, including sport, we hear a lot about personal image and personal brands. They are not nice terms to me because they project insincerity. Just the idea that you can create an image suggests that the image is not the real you. It's a manufactured version of you that has been formed to achieve a particular goal. However, in reality, image is very important because it is the way we are perceived by those who do not know us personally.

I had never been interested in mapping out what kind of brand or image I should have. I actually felt quite uncomfortable with that sort of talk. It was all just about playing cricket. But now that I have moved into the twilight of my career and have thought increasingly about things I want to do down the track, I have found it amazing how the perception of the way I went about my cricket is reflected in the way companies, the media and even governments perceive me, affecting the kinds of doors that open up afterwards.

There is plenty of proof that the players who had the best on-field image have ended up in interesting and enjoyable post-career positions. Adam Gilchrist played the game fairly and brilliantly, was respectful towards opponents and honourable in his role as a custodian of the baggy green. He was also a fierce competitor who was loyal and honest. He had a good sense of humour, was a good operator in a big room and was so down to earth he could talk to the average Joe or the prime minister. There is no doubt in my mind that Adam's image from his playing days set him up for a great future of opportunities in business, media and different organisations.

I like to think that the way I conducted myself on and off the field during my time in the spotlight was pretty good. I certainly have no regrets. I feel I came out of the game with a reputation that has made me attractive to various employers. Recently, I completed a two-year stint on the board of VenuesWest, a government board that looks after the interests of numerous government-owned sporting and entertainment venues in Perth.

For a while I wondered what VenuesWest wanted from me. I told the CEO that the extent of my knowledge of stadiums was the insides of dressing rooms and being out in the middle. I had no idea about catering, merchandise and all the sort of stuff that makes stadiums tick. The boss told me that they wanted me to give them a sportsman's view on what athletes need from venues and how best to cater for elite sporting events. I tried to learn as much as possible about the running of major venues, interaction with government, business and private stakeholders. It is a fascinating world I had never properly thought about and would never have been exposed to without having had a profile and reputation that VenuesWest saw as something they could use.

Additionally, I have in recent years taken on ambassador roles with the Commonwealth Bank, Brownes Dairy Company in WA, the emergency lighting company Clevertronics, and have been part of the Nine Network's cricket commentary team. These are roles I would never have been offered had I come out of the game with a poor reputation.

Exposing the real you

Increasingly, I believe, projecting a good image will become less about manufacturing an illusion and more about being a genuinely good person. Social media has ensured there is far less scope these days for getting away with being someone you are not. For instance, someone who designs an image as a well-behaved player but in fact behaves in an unacceptable way will be caught out by camera phones and exposed on social media. The pictures or stories will be tweeted or put on Facebook and there they will remain forever.

Fairly or not, mud sticks and it takes a lot of time and hard work to clean it off. Just ask Ricky Ponting. The future Australian captain got caught out early on after that infamous night at Kings Cross – and that was before social media. He had to work extremely hard for years afterwards to change people's perceptions of him. Once he became captain, especially, he really shaped up.

Ricky changed his behaviour, particularly around celebrating success and wins. He celebrated hard but whereas he would previously stay out all night partying, his new approach – which he stuck with through thick and thin – was to call stumps and go home to bed at a reasonable hour. Over time it changed the way he was perceived publicly and he ended his career as a revered Test batsman and skipper.

The circumstances and the times are different to Ricky's but I think David Warner has had a similar opportunity to change the way he is perceived publicly. From what I know of it, the Joe Root incident – where Dave was dropped from a Champions Trophy match in 2013 after a public skirmish with the England batsman – was blown out of proportion. But it must have been a great example to David that any such incident can take on a life of its own.

There are other instances when David made decisions that he maybe did not realise would have reverberations. One was when he faced the media after smashing an amazing hundred in a Test against India in Perth. I remember our media manager coming back to the dressing room shaking his head.

David had earlier said he did not want to talk to the press, and when told he had to he decided he would say a couple of crazy things. I just thought to myself, 'Oh, Dave, you don't realise that what you say now can be repeated for years to come. It's what you might be remembered for.'

David's rise to stardom was quick. He was a young and uncomplicated guy who was thrilled to have an opportunity and suddenly became a big star through his exciting performances. The change meant he had to make big adjustments in a short time, which is very difficult to do. The pressure of being scrutinised all the time is extremely heavy, anxiety and stress can build up and there can be a breaking point.

That is the hardest part about personal brands and image. Years and years can be spent building up a good reputation. But one mistake has the potential to set you back a long way.

Davey is close to his parents, has some very good close old friends and seems to have a happy private life these days. He is generous with his loved ones, flying them around to watch him play and helping them out where he can. He is a great character in the game and offers so much for fans. I think he has come a long way in understanding that the image he projects in and around cricket has a big effect on how he is perceived by millions of people around the world.

Stardom in a hurry

Ashton Agar is a terrific young man who I hope has a great future in the game as a left-arm orthodox bowler and decent lower-order batsman. But his remarkable experience of becoming a household name during the Ashes in 2013 was followed by a long period of treading water. And I was not the least bit surprised. His story is a striking example of how the glare of the spotlight can change the equation when you are trying to create a cricket career.

Ashton had played hardly any first-class cricket when he was thrown into the Test team and caught the attention of the nation by scoring a record 98 as the No.11 in the first Test at Trent Bridge. He said after the day's play: 'It's a dream come true ... Forever I've dreamed of playing Test cricket for Australia and for my debut to start the way it has, I'm over the moon.' But what he did not realise and was totally unprepared for was that suddenly the expectation and demands, on the ground and off it, would become enormous.

I captained Ashton in his first few games for WA. He bowled beautifully. He was accurate, had variation and could operate both aggressively and defensively. His batting was similar. He performed like any young guy coming into a new level of the game, without fear and with genuine excitement.

After just three first-class games the Australian selectors invited him on a national team tour to India to be a net bowler and gain experience from being around the team. It sounded like the right thing to do but the alarm bells went off for me immediately. I knew he would bowl really well, I knew the selectors had doubts over Nathan Lyon, despite investing eighteen months of hard work in him, and I had a sneaking suspicion they would see Ashton as the bolter who could fix everything.

Unsurprisingly Ashton turned heads while with the team in India. I remember getting a message from Steve Rixon saying,

'How good is this Ashton Agar? I think he should play the first Test in India.' I thought to myself, 'No way! Please don't make this mistake!' Ashton was nowhere near ready. In my opinion he needed three or four seasons of first-class cricket to learn and grow and have some idea of what he would be in for if he was to play Test cricket.

The selectors did not pick Ashton to play in India but he was thrown into the side for the first Ashes Test not long afterwards. I felt it was a huge mistake. Like in India, playing in the Ashes is akin to being in a cauldron. There are a multitude of distractions. There is so much hype and expectation. There are functions to go to, people to meet and huge interest from the media. There was no way this young fella could have been ready for that. For him to come out and score runs in his first match was a great achievement but it also created a perfect storm.

It's hard to comprehend how Ashton's life was turned upside down in the space of one day. I talked to him about it when he came back to Perth afterwards. He said he could not believe the interest in him following that innings. While walking down Kensington High Street with his girlfriend to do some shopping they were set upon by paparazzi. He said his girlfriend tried to run away, only to be chased by the photographers. He said he had no idea what to do. The two of them ended up locking themselves in the hotel room. Even as an experienced cricketer, that kind of attention is extremely hard to handle. But Ashton was a nineteen-year-old with hardly any cricketing experience. Suddenly he was being pursued as though he was a movie star.

For some time after the Ashes, Ashton was on a high while the public raved and the media loved him. But the wickets began to dry up. The harder he tried the worse he performed. He became frustrated and had too little experience to draw from to help him to change course. Eventually he got suspended in a match for showing dissent to an umpire. Ashton went from Ashes superstar to possible has-been in an alarmingly short time.

In my opinion the whole episode was very poorly handled. The duty of care to this young Australian cricketer was pretty much ignored. If everyone associated with making the decision to pick Ashton had just been patient and let him develop he would have held on to his youthful zeal, grown gradually in confidence, expanded his knowledge and been much better off in the long run. He could have made the regular mistakes that young guys do and worked his way through them away from the spotlight. He should have been given space to learn about bowling, learn about life and enjoy the maturing process.

I believe Ashton will come through this chastening experience and become a fantastic player. But I worry it will happen a lot later than it otherwise would have.

Ashton has a good head on his shoulders. He is intelligent and has good people around him. But my concern for young guys finding their way so publicly like he did is that they do not carry mental scars for the rest of their careers or throughout life. With the right help it is possible to come out of such situations a better person and a better cricketer. But for some people the negative effects can be enduring. Psychological damage can be deep and your outlook on the game can be changed forever.

Examples such as Ashton Agar and even Michael Clarke and others make me grateful for the path I travelled to get into international cricket. I have often said that I wished I had been picked earlier for Australia and learned on the job, making mistakes and progressing that way. But the more I have learned about life in the spotlight the more I feel lucky to have had the time to grow up at my own pace. Even after ten years of first-class cricket it was a very confronting adjustment to make when it all started to happen for me.

The importance of managers

Both at the time and in the weeks and months that followed Ashton Agar's ill-timed entry into international cricket, his manager, Jason Bakker, did his best to try to protect him from the many distractions that could divert him from concentrating on cricket. Commercial offers and opportunities came flooding in but Bakker was careful not to add to the already huge burden of trying to keep playing at the top level. It is a good illustration of the value of having a manager who has an understanding of life in the spotlight and the demands of first-class cricket.

In my early years playing for Western Australia, having a manager was pretty much discouraged. 'What do you need a manager for, Huss?' some of my older teammates would say. But my great mentor and coach at Northamptonshire, Bob Carter, had explained to me that it was a crucial piece in the puzzle of being prepared for top-level cricket.

Soon after I started playing county cricket Bob suggested I look at getting someone who could help me with all the requests and opportunities that he believed would come my way. 'I don't need a manager, Bob', I told him. To which he replied, 'You do need one. And you need someone you can trust because when you start playing for Australia everyone's going to want a piece of your time.' I never thought I would play for Australia, which made the whole manager thing seem pointless. But Bob was right about me playing for my country and he was also spot-on about choosing a manager very carefully.

Once I got into the Australian team and found myself in the public spotlight I was amazed how many people wanted my time. There were appearances to do here, charities to work with there, people left, right and centre wanting me to help them, talk to them, show up for them and just be around. In state cricket, too, there seemed to be an increasing number of requests and obligations each season. These days you can throw into the mix the T20 teams you represent and suddenly the balance becomes very difficult to manage. Picking the wrong manager in such an environment can be a terrible mistake.

Now more than ever financial opportunities for top cricketers come thick and fast and managers can often get lost in the temptation and steer players down the wrong path. I have heard many stories about managers pushing players into endorsements, shopping them around and exploiting them for money. The player becomes sidetracked from the primary goal, which is to stay focused on the core of it all – playing your best cricket.

I ended up meeting with Neil Maxwell, who not only knew the game of cricket, having played for NSW and Victoria, but also understood business, companies, brands and the media and knew how to build healthy relationships. I felt comfortable that Neil was someone who would respect that cricket remained my primary focus and opportunities outside the game would never take precedence. Neil had just a handful of clients, which suggested to me we could have a good friendly relationship rather than work at a distance. It would allow Neil to learn that my personality was not about chasing every commercial deal that could be squeezed out of my career. Rather, I wanted to have the distractions removed as much as possible so I could concentrate on my cricket.

THE FORMS OF THE GAME

A different game

In 2008, shortly after my first book, *Driven to Succeed*, was published, the IPL started and almost immediately turned the game on its head. The glitzy and glamorous Twenty20 competition sparked a modernisation of the entire sport. Suddenly players could represent clubs or franchises instead of states and nations, a monumental change from well over a century of tradition. Big money was up for grabs. With private ownership, often by celebrities or very successful businesspeople, the players were able to make money their predecessors could only have dreamed about.

The IPL spread opportunities for players more widely. Where previously just a handful of people from each nation could get a chance to play on the big stage, now there were eight squads in India and a host of others in other nations where T20 competitions later sprang up. Whatever reservations conservatives may have had, there was no denying the emergence of this new and brash form of the game and its revolutionary competition structure. The Establishment was left with no choice but to work within a new system, and administrators could no longer rest on their laurels.

This period of upheaval is still very much in motion and no one can say with certainty what the final outcomes will be. The fifty-over game was the subject of much conjecture before T20 came along and is arguably more so now. Test cricket was under pressure in some parts of the world during the 1990s and early 2000s. Some might argue it's healthier now in some places, while in others it's in real strife. Either way the seismic shift T20 has caused is still producing aftershocks and will for some time.

While I acknowledge that T20 has affected cricket negatively in some parts of the world, I believe that overall it has had a positive effect on the game. Perhaps its biggest achievement has been beyond the boundary rope. T20 has exposed millions more people to cricket. Its three-hour duration in a world in which many people are time poor or seek instant gratification has enticed legions of new fans. Among them have been families, women and youngsters who might have ended up following or playing other sports. Right from the start the hope was that these new T20 fans would eventually come to follow fifty-over cricket and ultimately Test cricket. It's hard to quantify but my gut feeling is that this seems to be happening. In Australia, at least, all three forms of the game are flourishing and the national team is the most popular sporting team in the country.

On the field there is no denying that T20 has had a huge impact. Like most players who were around at the top level when it emerged, I originally saw the new format as little more than fun or even just a gimmick. It was designed purely to entertain crowds and the players enjoyed getting out there in a light-hearted environment to have a bash. It was quite nice to play a brand of the game in which you were not under a lot of pressure and could show your skills. Whether you succeeded or not hardly mattered.

Even at the IPL that first year there seemed more of an emphasis on fun than serious competition. We felt no pressure to do anything other than try to hit sixes off every ball. Training was lax, tactics did not really matter and there was none of the kind of intensity or scrutiny that we all were used to in our everyday careers as professional players. Instead, the early IPL was more about lavish parties, big names and lots of colour and excitement. There was a sense, to me, that decades of pent-up frustration in world cricket was suddenly released and everyone wanted to celebrate.

That early environment did not last long. The IPL quickly became a very serious competition in which every team is desperate to win. Clubs nowadays are genuinely big businesses and are run as such, with performance indicators and accomplished personnel. For unheralded players there are wonderful new opportunities to be involved in a major competition and make a good living in the process. For more well-known players there are reputations and contracts to protect and improve upon.

Form in T20 is not just incidental anymore. It very much means something and national selectors keep an eye on what is going on. Players want to be part of their national T20 sides and play in the T20 World Cup, and performing well in the IPL is a credible way of earning a spot. Coaches and support staff, too, are accountable and see their chances to make an impression across the board and establish or develop their careers. The professionalism of clubs, team structures, training and tactics has grown enormously in just a few years. That credibility has filtered through to all the other T20 competitions that have emerged and lifted standards in the sport as a whole.

Breaking down barriers

One of the biggest changes that club-based Twenty20 competitions have brought about is that players come from all over the world to form teams. In our Chennai side for the 2015 IPL there were five nationalities represented. While this poses challenges such as coordinating preparation and fostering a strong team spirit, it also has, I believe, brought the cricketing family closer together.

Playing in different T20 competitions has given us all the opportunity to learn so much about cricket around the world and also about different cultures. I could talk to guys from the West Indies about the state of the game there or talk to guys from India about how they play spin. It's a unique chance to learn about different life philosophies and opinions and make friends with people from various countries.

Sometimes it takes a little while to strike up friendships with your teammates. In nation-based international cricket often there are particular players who act like opposite ends of a magnet. They just rub each other up the wrong way. Kieron Pollard, for example, had several run-ins with Australian players over the years, including David Warner and James Faulkner.

I did not know what to expect when I met Kieron when we played together for the Mumbai Indians. But I was pleased to find he was a really nice guy. He was great company and offered me a lot of lessons in the way he went about his cricket. I would never have come to properly know Kieron had it not been for T20.

In conversation with Kieron, as well as another West Indian player in the Mumbai team, Krishmar Santokie, I discovered that the image they had of us Australian players was that we were all the same – very aggressive and unpleasant, even nasty at times. Kieron kept a bit of a distance from me at first, probably for that very reason. It took some weeks to break down the barrier and convince him that not all of us Aussies are the same. Sure, there are some guys who come off as quite aggressive or unpleasant. But just like in any team from any part of the world, there are different characters and personalities.

I had a similar experience with Santokie. On a bus trip once, he said, 'What is it with you Aussies? Why do you have to sledge all the time and say nasty things about your opponents?' I went through the same conversation with him, telling him that, yes, there were some guys in Australian cricket who go over the top, but the majority of us play hard and fair. We are not all the same. I think Kieron and Krishmar learned a bit more about Australia and Australians by getting to know me and I think that can only be a good thing.

The IPL allows people to be themselves and not be judged on the reputations of others or on incidents that might have happened in games between countries. There are a few cases of players being brought together after having been sworn enemies.

A good example is Ricky Ponting and Harbhajan Singh, who have a lot of history from their days as Test and one-day combatants. Now Ricky coaches Harbhajan at Mumbai and the pair get along quite well and have a productive working relationship.

I think the breaking down of barriers, while being a positive development in general, has probably been more of an advantage for some other national teams than for Australia. Over the past twenty years or so Australian teams have been able to build up something of an aura of invincibility, which was used to great effect to get a psychological edge over opponents. However, by being in the same change room, staying in the same hotels and playing in the same teams as players from here, there and everywhere, that aura has diminished.

I will never forget the looks on the faces of some of the Chennai players when Matthew Hayden turned up for season one of the IPL. To see some of them, especially the less established players, literally cowering in fear when he walked in was quite a sight. It was because of the dominating persona Matthew had built up over years of hard Test and one-day cricket. The players in that room had either played against Matthew or heard about his aggression, sledging and mind games on the field and were scared of him. 'G'day! How are you going?' Matthew bellowed when he walked into the room that first day, sporting a big warm smile. Within a little while the players came to realise he was a terrific bloke and there was nothing to fear. It was great for them. But in terms of Australia's quest to keep its mental edge in international competition, it probably was not ideal.

Relationships take time to build, especially with players you may have been in heated battle with just a short time earlier.

But the environment is conducive to personal links being established just like they are within a state or national team. We all – including the local Indian players – stay at the same hotel for the duration of the tournament. We have our own team room, where we hold our team meetings and spend time together. There are pool and table tennis tables, TVs and gaming consoles. You can lounge around on beanbags and chat and you end up having meals with just about everyone in the squad at some point. We train together every day and work up towards games together in the same way a state or national team does. In some cities you cannot go out among the public very often so you end up spending a lot of time together with your teammates in the hotel.

Over the eight weeks of the tournament it's pretty much impossible not to become friendly with particular people in the team. When you come back the following season it's great to catch up again and slot back in with those teammates. There is less chance of the kind of staleness that can come from touring with the same group over and over in a national team, travelling around and socialising with the same guys each day, because you are only in the IPL environment for a few weeks each year. I find it quite exciting to have that change of pace, a genuine change of atmosphere with a real international flavour.

Same game, different priorities

Of course, not everything is straightforward when it comes to playing in a side featuring players from around the world. At the Champions League in 2014 our Mumbai Indians side performed quite poorly overall and our owners – who were some of the richest people in India and not used to losing – met with us to express their disappointment. They said words to the effect that we had let down their brand, did not show pride and had not looked like we were playing as a team.

After they left, the players had a chat and agreed that it had been a disappointing time. We had let down ourselves, the fans and the owners. But there was also a sense that some of their comments were out of touch with the reality of the circumstances. We had players in that team from numerous countries, different cultures and playing environments. This diverse group had come together just a handful of days before the tournament started. We felt it had been unrealistic for the owners to expect that we would be able to forge the kind of team spirit and camaraderie that might exist in a team of mates playing for their country. In fact, in any T20 team, while players will certainly try their hardest to perform well and win matches, it's a fantasy to think you are going to feel the same strong sense of togetherness that is found in a successful national team.

One big disparity that can exist among the players is their priorities. T20 has a much more individualistic aspect to it compared with playing for a national side, where the priority is overwhelmingly about doing what is best for the team and, therefore, the country. There are several players I have come across in T20 who are striking examples of the modern mercenary-style player in that they probably place a greater importance on their personal performances than some other players.

In any team, be it a Test team or a T20 franchise, a loss will be somewhat softened for an individual if they have produced an outstanding personal performance. It's just human nature. However, in T20 particularly, the balance is skewed towards individuals trying to ensure that their personal value is maintained or increased. This aspect of the T20 culture, the free-agent mentality, has given many players the belief that as long as they are getting the numbers on the board personally they will progress regardless of how the team is going. You would have to say the evidence proves they are right.

I believe it's unfair to judge players harshly for feeling more concerned about their personal performances than, say, I do. Cricketers are each at different stages of their careers and have different goals. A player just starting out is probably going to place more importance on performing well personally at a T20 tournament than one who has played fifty Tests and has nothing much else to prove.

I think one of the major reasons we have seen this pattern be exacerbated along national lines is because cricketers playing for their country in places like the West Indies, Sri Lanka and New Zealand are paid much less than we are in Australia. Established Australian players do not necessarily need to play T20 to make a good living whereas, say, for West Indians, T20 offers them far and away their best chance of setting themselves and their families up. Therefore, I think, it makes sense that some players, especially those from places where the central contracts are not worth as much, will feel a greater sense of achievement from personal success in a losing side than some others might.

The West Indies

The emergence of T20 has exposed deficiencies within national structures and forced them to seek ways to fix their problems.

This is nowhere more obvious than in the current crisis affecting the West Indies. So much has changed since my early days growing up watching the likes of Malcolm Marshall, Viv Richards, Joel Garner, Richie Richardson and a host of other Caribbean cricketers dominate the game. They were the world's best in Tests and one-dayers, mastering both with flair and skill. Their brilliance inspired countless others to become involved in the game, either as participants or viewers, and set the benchmark for cricketing excellence.

Today West Indies cricket is in no-man's-land. No longer are opposing batsmen trying to survive their fast bowling onslaughts or incredible strokeplay. Rather, the game itself is battling for survival in that wonderful part of the world as changing priorities and attitudes split what once appeared to be an unshakeable foundation.

If it turns out that Test and one-day cricket fade away in the Caribbean it would be a real tragedy. Let us hope that does not happen. But whatever the outcome, I believe the challenges facing West Indies cricket offer useful lessons about how the foundations of the game need to be protected in a rapidly changing cricketing environment.

I think it's fair to say that T20 has had more of an impact on cricket in the West Indies than anywhere else. Almost all the West Indian cricketers I have come across love the short game. They thrive on the idea of coming into a rock and roll–style environment, smashing the ball as hard as possible and getting out of there. The crux of the problem, however, is that many West Indian players end up becoming more dedicated to T20 than playing internationally.

When you delve a bit deeper it becomes easier to understand why it's happening and harder to blame the players for taking the approach they do. So much of the small talk I have heard from West Indian players over the years has been about the awful hotels they stay in, the difficult scheduling they face and the small and unreliable earnings they receive. Their complaints can sound monotonous. But when you consider there are so many players saying the same sorts of things, you start to realise they must have a point.

I feel I cannot blame those West Indian players who end up becoming highly motivated to do well in T20 club competitions instead of putting their national team aspirations first. If players are being treated poorly by their employers and more attractive avenues become available, of course they will gravitate in that direction. West Indies cricketers see T20 as a way to bypass their governing body and conduct their careers much more freely. T20 gives them the ability to run their own show for the most part, have fun and be paid well. They avoid being responsible to a poorly run system in which they are poorly rewarded.

I don't believe it's fair for Australian players, or the public for that matter, to negatively judge West Indian players, such as Kieron Pollard, who choose to become T20-only players, because Australian cricketers, by comparison, are very well looked after by Cricket Australia. A lot of money comes into our governing body from broadcast deals and sponsorships and a generous percentage of it is passed on to the players. The entire elite level of Australian cricketers are well paid, travel comfortably and have a big say in what goes on around them. They are treated with respect. Professional cricketers in Australia are mostly happy and have few obstacles to achieving their best. The game in Australia, in short, is run very well. It is one of the main reasons Test cricket in Australia remains strong and positively rather than negatively affected by the rise of T20.

Issues around wages, scheduling and the like have been around for decades. However, they never seriously affected the health of the game overall. The emergence of T20 has put the game's leaders everywhere on notice that they need to lift their performance, especially in places like the West Indies, where they seem to have dropped the ball sometime ago.

Twenty20's on-field revolution

Just as the effects of T20 off the field will continue to reverberate, I think its influence on the field has been enormous and will continue to evolve and affect the way the game is played. In much the same way one-day cricket inspired changes to the way in which Test cricket was played, T20 has taken aspects of the game to a new level, sometimes to levels people thought impossible, sending waves of innovation right through the three forms.

Batting has been revolutionised by T20. Players have come up with shots no one could have imagined just a few years ago. There are switch hits, under scoops and reverse slogs, and batsmen are using the crease like never before. Bowlers have become highly innovative and developed new weapons such as slow bouncers, wide yorkers and a variety of differently paced deliveries. They are more disciplined now too. Bowlers are under enormous pressure every time they run up to the crease. A no-ball can be incredibly costly as it means a free hit and another delivery. Anything too short, too full or too wide will probably end up being smashed out of the ground. Bowlers have to execute perfectly, and the best ones do.

Fielding standards have gone through the roof. The dynamic South African Jonty Rhodes set a benchmark for fielding in the 1990s, but these days it seems like every team has several players of Jonty's calibre. Ground fielding, catching and supporting each other in the field have all developed incredibly. In T20 cricket you always have to be thinking, innovating and working out ways to get ahead of the rest. I find it thrilling and very challenging.

At the 2015 fifty-over World Cup we saw how the advancements T20 has brought about have transferred across to the one-day game and made it so much more exciting. At the World Cup there were twenty-eight team totals over 300 – at the 2003 World Cup, two years before the IPL began, there were just nine. In 2015, there were three team scores over 400 – there were fifteen in the entire forty-four-year history of one-day cricket before that. There were thirty-eight centuries scored, including four in a row by Sri Lanka's Kumar Sangakkara, and two players, West Indian Chris Gayle and New Zealander Martin Guptill, hit double hundreds. Gayle hit twenty-six sixes in the tournament, across which the average scoring rate was an extraordinary 5.65 per over. A whole host of batsmen scored big runs at strike rates far in excess of 100. It was like nothing we had ever seen before and I have no doubt that T20 was behind a lot of this change.

The scores suggest that the bowling was substandard. But I do not believe it was. The skills required to bowl well in T20 have clearly come across to fifty-over cricket. I thought

Mitchell Starc was brilliant throughout the tournament. His pace, accuracy and swing earned a haul of twenty-two wickets at a stunning average of just 10.18. Kiwi paceman Trent Boult was right up there too, with twenty-two wickets at 16.86. These two fast bowlers can lay claim to having spearheaded their respective teams into the final as much as any batsman could. There were a number of unforgettable spells in the tournament, including New Zealander Tim Southee's brilliant 7–33 against England and Pakistan's Wahab Riaz's fiery battle with Shane Watson in the quarterfinal.

It's not only one-day cricket that has been given a kick-along by T20. I think its influence has filtered right through to the Test arena. Batting strike rates and team run rates have gone through the roof in the five-day game. There are fewer draws than ever as teams look to attack and employ unusual tactics to take wickets, score faster and gain the upper hand.

Purists might argue that the increased speed at which the Test game is played has taken some of the endurance and concentration skills out of the equation. There is certainly some merit to that point of view as batsmen are perhaps less skilled at building long innings and bowlers are less patient at working batsmen out. However, I think the positives of attacking, innovative and quicker Test cricket make the game much more attractive and appropriate for the times we live in. This sort of progress outweighs the drawbacks.

Twenty20 as a career starter

The crossover of influences from T20 to the other forms of the game has had a bearing on the way players can establish themselves. I used to think that to be a highly regarded T20 player you had to have first proven yourself in one-day or Test cricket. I thought that T20 would remain the domain of the top echelon of players and could be seen as a bit of a reward for success elsewhere. But that has been shown not to be the case. Whereas once Test and one-day cricket were the avenues into the world of T20, more recently, eye-catching performances in the shortest game have led to opportunities for players in the Test and one-day teams.

In David Warner's early days he was pigeonholed as a slogger, a bit of a rent-a-six, and not a serious batsman in the traditional sense. He was an early victim of the stigma that T20 carried as being a hit-and-giggle type of contest. But that perception has changed and with it came a change to the ideas about David's potential to play the other forms. As we have seen, David has transformed himself from a T20 slogger into a successful, exciting and somewhat revolutionary batsman in all three forms of the game.

I think in the future we will see more players making their way from T20 into the one-day and Test sides, in the way that Glenn Maxwell and Aaron Finch are now. These guys could have gone down the path of being T20 specialists and made millions of dollars travelling the world without ever playing international cricket. However, like the overwhelming majority of Australian cricketers, their goals are to have big international careers representing their country in Test cricket. That players such as Warner, Finch and Maxwell have used T20 as a launching pad into one-day and Test cricket raises the credibility of T20 as a style of the game that takes great skill and application.

I don't think we should be too surprised by the T20-first model. It's a similar evolution to that which we saw when fifty-over cricket emerged and good form in the one-day team led to Test selection. It's how my Test career began. The point is, it is no longer a case of taking the route in one direction, it's now a two- (or three-) way street and a case of showing you can perform on the big stage no matter what form of the game it's in.

Corruption

Unfortunately, you cannot talk about the pros and cons of Twenty20 cricket without considering what is surely the greatest potential drawback of all. If we are not able to stamp out the kind of corruption that has become a nasty bedfellow of T20, I, along with many others, fear the ramifications could be dire. Nothing is more important in any sport than its integrity.

Corruption has been part of cricket since well before T20. But there is no doubt that the shortest form of the game has all the ingredients to make it a prime target for criminals who prey on vulnerable players. Its hurly-burly nature, unpredictability and lack of structure, the movement of players between teams and the belief by some that results are not as important as in international cricket – each of these factors has the capacity to create an environment in which problems with integrity can arise.

I believe that 99 per cent of players involved today in T20 competitions around the world are not involved in any form of corruption. But that is irrelevant. Even if only a tiny number of players are doing the wrong thing it's enough to destroy the sport from within because players and fans alike start to wonder if any of the amazing things that happen during a game are actually genuine or a set-up.

I have played T20 basically since the start and have never been approached by bookmakers or criminals and never been subjected to or caught up in anything illegal. But what I can say is this: I have seen numerous things happen on the field while I have been playing that have left me scratching my head. How did that just happen? Why did that guy go for a suicidal second run? How could that fieldsman drop such a simple catch? Why did that bowler just send down yet another no-ball? I have tried to dismiss these concerns but maybe I am too trusting or naive. Other players I have spoken to have felt certain that some things they have seen on the field are examples of players taking cash for favours.

I have thought a lot about what types of players are open to corruption and have come to realise that it is not as simple as saying it is just bad guys. It's far more complex than that. The more I have learned about who gets caught up in these situations the more I have come to have some sympathy for them. For instance, imagine you are a young Sri Lankan, West Indian or New Zealand cricketer and are being paid a pittance on one of the low-end contracts as you put everything into gaining a national contract. A man approaches you at one of the many IPL functions. He tells you that if you bowl just one or two no-balls at particular times he will ensure you are paid three times your entire yearly wage. What would you do? Yes, of course it's the wrong thing to do and contrary to everything we are taught about honesty and integrity. But you would stop and think about it, surely. Any person would.

The big problem with accepting such an offer is that it looks good at the time but it almost immediately makes you a prisoner to the person or group who initiated the deal. Criminal organisations have long tentacles and spend plenty of time and effort trapping their targets in webs of blackmail and deceit. They will infiltrate playing groups, starting small by perhaps offering small amounts of cash for small pieces of information. Who will be selected for the next game? What will be the batting order? Who will open the bowling? It seems innocuous at the time. But once a player accepts one payment he is at the mercy of the criminal element because his secret can never be revealed. If it is revealed his career will likely be over. If not his career, his reputation, surely, is shot. The hole deepens and the player might never be able to escape. It must be an extremely stressful way to live and play cricket.

T20 seems ripe for corruption. But it is not the only form of the game in which players can be caught up doing the wrong thing. In the same way I have felt some sympathy for players targeted by criminals in T20, I felt for Mohammad Amir, the young Pakistan player who bowled preplanned no-balls in a Test match in England in 2011 and was subsequently sent to prison after it emerged he was part of a spot-fixing scam. I could not help thinking about what I would have done if, as a teenager in the Australian team, Ricky Ponting ordered me to bowl a no-ball on the third ball of my next over. All sorts of thoughts would have gone through my mind. *I shouldn't do it. But if I don't, I'll be double-crossing my captain and will probably never play for my country again.* What would you do? Corruption is a very difficult and complex problem.

Tackling the problem

Thankfully, in recent years the threat of corruption has been taken very seriously and genuine effort is going into educating players about the dangers. Each year at T20 tournaments, just like in the national team structure, players are required to attend workshops and formal meetings where experts in the field talk about the warning signs, dangers and possible scenarios. This is a positive step. However, I have long felt frustrated that so little seems to be done about catching the perpetrators, those syndicates, bookmakers and criminals who see a fertile ground in cricket for making illegal money.

I remember at one of these workshops, before the T20 World Cup in Sri Lanka in 2012, the International Cricket Council (ICC) Integrity Unit people went through the talk about the pitfalls and warning signs of corruption. I decided to speak up. 'This is all well and good', I said. 'But what are you guys actually doing to catch these crooks?' My point was that it felt unfair to me that the onus always seemed to be on the players to resist the temptations rather than on the authorities to catch the people causing the problem in the first place. 'Are we only going to catch these people when there is a newspaper sting?' I asked. 'What is being done to put a stop to this stuff?'

The reply answered my question but hardly alleviated my frustration. I was told that the resources simply were not there to operate like detectives and go after the criminal syndicates. The best way to stop the rot, the ICC said, was to put an end to the supply chain at the players' end. That involved constant education, regular and accurate flow of information and sufficient communication among nations, teams and tournament organisers. Beyond that there had to be strong penalties to act as deterrents so that the temptation for players to infringe is diminished.

With these measures in place you would hope that the incidence of problems is lessened. Isolated incidents will still occur, I am almost certain. But if it is drummed into players enough, they will see that by falling into this trap, they are risking their livelihoods, reputations and careers. They are also deeply injuring the game itself.

If the temptation to cheat like this ever comes the way of a young cricketer – or athlete in any sport – my advice would be to consider how it ended up for the Indian bowler Sreesanth, who received a life ban from the BCCI in 2013. Nearly everyone these days, at just the mention of his name, thinks 'spot fixer'. Sadly, even though his case was thrown out of court in 2015, I can no longer think of Sreesanth as an extremely good out-swing bowler for India. His reputation, unfortunately, is tainted forever. This is what every player risks by letting criminals infiltrate their cricket. I hope all players get that message and never forget it.

The one-day game

As much as I have come around to Twenty20 as a serious, important and exciting brand of cricket I will always have a special place in my heart for the fifty-over game for two main reasons. Firstly, it's where my international journey began, when we played a really strong India side in Perth back in early 2004. After many years of hard work I finally had the chance to represent my country on my home ground in front of my family and friends and was part of the final partnership with my old mate from WA, Simon Katich, in what was to be a five-wicket win. The second reason is that I believe fifty-over cricket is simply a great game.

Whereas T20 does and will likely always favour power-hitting batsmen, super-fast bowlers and exceptional fielders, one-day cricket calls for a wider variety of skills. You need quicks and mediums and a good spinner. You need dashing batsmen, finishers and a guy or two who can bat through an innings. Where I mostly batted throughout my one-day career, in the late middle order, I never knew what I would be faced with. I could come in at 3–10 and have to resurrect the innings over the next couple of hours. I could come in for the last ten overs and have to lift the run rate. I could have to bat with the tail and need to take the lead. There were so many different situations that could arise and for which I had to be prepared.

Throughout play more variations can occur in fifty-over cricket than T20. In the shortest form of the game the result can be all but determined in the first few overs of the match. If Chris Gayle, for instance, blazes away for the opening five or six overs it's just about goodnight for the team batting second. Similarly if you get him and a couple of his teammates out early you may have pretty much sewn up the result inside the first half an hour. It's very hard to change the complexion of the game from the early pace. The same cannot be said of one-day cricket, where there is much more time to formulate a comeback and reverse the early trend. It raises the possibility for absorbing seesawing contests.

We have seen so many amazing feats achieved in one-dayers. I will never forget the reaction when John Buchanan, the coach of what was a great Australian team, challenged us to score 400 in an innings. We laughed at him and told him he was dreaming. Yet he maintained that we had the talent to do the unthinkable and take the game to a new level. Sure enough, on our next tour to South Africa, in March 2006 in a match at Johannesburg, we made 434, a run-rate of 8.68 sustained for nearly four hours. Ricky Ponting cracked an amazing 164 from 105 balls, Adam Gilchrist and Simon Katich made half centuries and I got in on the act with 81 from 51 balls. Everyone could see the 'I told you so' look on John's face afterwards. It was priceless. Incredibly, the most remarkable thing about that day was that we lost! South Africa knocked over the total with a ball to spare. You can never predict what will happen in a game of fifty-over cricket.

Another great strength of the fifty-over game is the World Cup. For all players, I believe, one of the key pillars to the attractiveness of one-day cricket is the lure of playing in a tournament that, aside from the biggest Test tours and series, is the most cherished event a cricketer can be involved in. I certainly loved my experiences in that tournament and count one of my greatest achievements as being part of a World Cup–winning team.

World Cups are special because you are playing against all the best players in the world at one time. Everyone is there together, aiming for the same prize. To come out on top is a feeling unlike any other in the game. Perhaps in years to come they will count World T20s as equally or even more prestigious. But in my experience the fifty-over tournament is as good as it gets.

Whatever the future holds for T20, however big it becomes or however strong the club-based system grows, I am adamant that fifty-over cricket will continue to hold an important place. I believe boards and administrators want it to remain successful because it is a very lucrative product with advertisements, sponsorships and broadcast rights used across seven hours of play rather than three. But I think, more importantly, players and fans will continue to love the game for its great skills, challenges and unpredictability.

Test match cricket – the ultimate

The third form of the game, Test cricket – the original game of cricket – is, in my opinion and many others', the pinnacle of our sport. It is the realm in which you are truly judged by your colleagues and opponents. It is the place where you gain your respect. It is where reputations can be dashed or become legendary.

When you are on the cusp of a big Test series the level of hype is different to anything else in the game. One-day matches and Twenty20 games and tournaments can excite fans but they never command the general public's attention like an Ashes series or an India tour. There is so much interest and discussion around the game and the team, so much media, so many functions and official engagements to attend. It only adds to an already heightened level of excitement about what lies ahead.

Test cricket is challenging in every way – technically, tactically, physically, mentally. You are challenged from within and without. You are placed under extreme pressure and asked to come up with answers. If you are a real competitor there is no place you would rather be than representing your country in the rough and tumble of a Test match struggle. And there is no better feeling than prevailing in an exam on the hardest levels against the best possible players. Test match wins are times to feel proud of your efforts, abilities, preparation, application and, perhaps above all, your character.

Nearly all of us have spoken to noncricketing people who ask 'How can you play a game for five days and not get a result?' My response is always that it's not just about the result. It's about the journey. A Test match is like going on a theme park ride. There are ups and downs, tricks and bumps. There are fast patches and lulls. There are moments of high excitement and opportunity, others of endurance and patience. It is a test of all states of mind.

The conditions change. The pitch evolves and different bowlers and batsmen come into the game. A big fast bowler will dominate day one; a rearguard action from a middle order batsman becomes the story of day two. By day five the spinners are churning up a cracked pitch and the tale twists again. There is so much drama over the five days. Every Test match tells a story and each participant is part of that story.

To me, Test cricket is such a perfect form of competition that it's hard to accept that the game faces enormous challenges to stay relevant and attractive. In my experience, England and South Africa maintain a strong attachment to the five-day game. I would question whether the same can be said of the subcontinental countries and West Indies. For the moment, I believe the majority of current players will continue to hold Test cricket as the ultimate. But when you have certain elite players deciding to forgo their Test careers to play T20 full time, it makes me a bit nervous about the next generation.

In Australia, for the moment, Test cricket is thriving. Australia has been among the best nations at keeping pride at the core of our regard for Test matches. A lot of it has stemmed from our reverence for the baggy green. The deep-green cap is held in esteem unlike any other piece of sporting attire, kept as a reward for only the very best cricketers in the land. I think Steve Waugh has a lot to be proud of for having helped reignite the cap's history, tradition and spirit throughout the 1990s and beyond, and keeping Test cricket at the centre of our love for the game.

Moving between the three forms

I believe there is an appetite for all three forms of the game to remain successful well into the future. But the challenge for players good enough to play all three is only going to get harder. After my 50th Test, against New Zealand in Hamilton, I went straight to India, where I joined up with the Super Kings. The tournament was already underway and I found it nearly impossible to slot into that very different mode. Rather than looking to strike the ball, as you must in T20, I was trying to stroke the ball as you do in longer forms. I was scoring at about a run a ball, which does not cut it in T20. Eventually I was dropped from the side and it took more than two weeks of hard work in the nets to get into the swing of things.

The Australian Cricketers' Association in their State of the Game Report started to look at the issues of players going quickly from one form of the game to another and hopefully in the future there will be improvements to the way games are scheduled so it is more manageable. For instance, in an Australian summer, if there are Test matches taking place around the time of the Big Bash League, how can players push their claims for Test selection? If there is an injury to a player in the Test team, should a replacement be brought in straight from a Big Bash team? It's a very big ask for someone to go from playing for the Sydney Thunder or Brisbane Heat to batting at No.4 or 5 in the Test side just a few days later. It would make more sense for there to be Sheffield Shield games scheduled during Test series and one-day domestic cricket while there are international one-dayers being played.

Maybe the demands of moving between all three forms of the game will prove too great. Even when I was playing there was only a handful of us playing all forms – Brad Haddin, Shane Watson, Mitchell Johnson, Brett Lee and me. I suspect there will be less crossover in the future. I found the sheer physical and mental burden too difficult to play all the cricket on offer. However, as we have seen over and over, cricket keeps proving the doubters wrong. The game and its participants continue to adapt in ways most of us never thought possible.

Rick McCosker coming out to bat with a broken jaw in the Centenary Test in 1977, Shane Warne bowling for two sessions nonstop on the last day of the Ashes Test in Adelaide in 2006, Ricky Ponting scoring a hundred in each innings in his 100th Test and a couple of matches later Justin Langer getting knocked out first ball in his 100th – cricket works in mysterious ways. But it is not only in Tests that the magic of our game comes to the fore. What about the impossible miraculous limited-overs wins? At the IPL in 2013 we needed to score 198 in 14.3 overs. It was one of those equations that should have been simply impossible. No one gave us a chance. Yet we hit a six off the last ball to win. It was another miracle provided by the game we love. Miracles? Sachin Tendulkar played 200 Test matches. How can that be? How does someone play even 100 Test matches, let alone 200? The 434 game in South Africa – in which we got beaten. The list goes on and on. Cricket delivers mind-blowing outcomes that keep millions of us enthralled. It will continue to do that in all three forms of the game for a long time to come.

THE INTERNATIONAL WORLD

First experiences

Cricket was the catalyst for my first trip out of Perth and also my first trip overseas. They were very different sorts of trips. When I was selected in the Western Australia under 17s I was so excited about heading out of town to represent the state and going to a new environment to play my favourite sport with a bunch of young blokes I enjoyed being around. We went all the way to sunny Canberra. What could be better?

My next trip, to India, was something very different and the first instalment in what would be a long education in the wonders of the international world. Unlike my later experiences travelling with the Australian team, on that first trip to India we stayed in three-star hotels, flew economy class in packed aircraft, looked after our own bags and all became terribly sick. It was an unforgettable introduction to the exciting and challenging privilege of travelling to play cricket.

It began back in 1994, when I was playing in the WA under 19s team at the national carnival in Melbourne. On the final night of the tournament, which WA happened to win, they announced the Australian under 19s squad to travel to India to play 'Test matches' and one-dayers.

I was desperate to be selected and thought I was an outside chance, having had a decent tournament. I tried not to think about it too much because I did not want to be too disappointed if I missed out. When they read out the final list they named three openers in the squad and I was one of them. I could not believe it. It was a very strong squad consisting of several future stars, including Brett Lee and Andrew Symonds. Jason Gillespie joined the team later as a replacement.

It was a surreal feeling to be named and I was very proud to be able to represent my country on the cricket field for the first time. After getting back home to Perth I had two months to wait before we left and thoughts started whizzing through my mind about what to expect. I was quite daunted by the prospect of going to a mysterious country like India, especially having never ventured outside Australia.

Cricket-wise I wondered if I was really up to standard. Would I fit into my team? Could I take on the Indian young guns? What would the conditions be like? How could I prepare for it all? Beyond the cricket I wondered about the heat, the food, the day-to-day living. *How will I communicate with people over there? What happens if I get sick? What do I have to do to make sure I'm polite and don't offend any of the locals?* This was going to be a lot more complex than heading over to Canberra or Melbourne!

We arrived in Chennai, or Madras as it was then, late at night and the first thing that struck me was the sheer number of people who were out and about. The airport was full and outside I was stunned by the sight of entire families on the side of the road. It was hot, humid and uncomfortable and there seemed to be people everywhere lying on the pavement, lots of them beggars who came up to our team bus asking for money. We had never seen anything like it.

Upon arriving at the hotel we found it to be architecturally beautiful but very old. It had a genuine colonial feel to it with four-post beds and marble floors. It seemed like something out of an old movie or a good book. I was exhausted after hours of adrenaline pumping through me and decided to rest. I believed I could just switch on the following day after a good sleep in a half-decent bed.

It turned out to be a bit harder than that. In fact it took about two or three training sessions before I was able to properly switch my mind on to the task we had ahead of us. I think everyone was a bit on edge, wondering how we would gel as a team and how we would all adapt to the environment we were in, an environment that felt about as foreign as possible.

Our first game was at a crappy old ground somewhere outside of Hyderabad, where our dressing room was a few wooden posts with a sheet over the top. I went out to bat with fellow West Australian Justin Cantrell, told him I would take the first ball of the tour and was clean bowled for a golden duck. Yep, the first ball I ever faced outside of Australia, on a dusty old ground somewhere on the outskirts of a big Indian city, crashed into my stumps and sent me on my way.

For someone who was not the most confident person in the world it was hardly the ideal start to my international playing days. I supposed my teammates thought I was hopeless, the opposition thought I was an easy target and the coaches might just get rid of me. Thinking back, of course, it was just one ball, one innings and really nothing too dire. But at the time all I could think was that I was in a strange place, there were strange people everywhere, strange food, hot humid conditions and I had been cleaned up for a first ball globe. It was a very confronting situation.

We were to have one more warm-up game before contesting three youth Tests and three one-dayers over eight weeks. It felt like the longest eight weeks of our lives and I think we were all excited to get home at the end. Looking back, however, that trip will linger in all of our memories as one of the greatest experiences of our lives.

Part of what makes travelling so unforgettable is not just the good times, but also the bad times. One of the reasons that first trip to India was so memorable was the dramas that arose, not least the instances of players becoming ill. The funniest one was the Victorian Chris Burton during a game in Bangalore. He was running in to bowl and as he was about to jump he said, 'Nah, can't jump', kept running past the umpire, past the batsman, straight off the field, up the stairs to the dressing room and into the toilets. We all thought it was hilarious.

Chris was not the first player to get sick. That honour fell to Brett Lee only a few days into the trip. He had been in the shower and, as he said he always did, started taking in gulps of water as he stood there. He said at the time that he took one big gulp and as he took the second realised where he was and that he was in trouble. Sure enough within only one hour he was sick and out of action for a good couple of days.

I thought I definitely would not fall for such a mistake. After all, Brett was just a fast bowler with not much going on upstairs and I was a smart young batsman. But eventually I had my turn too. Between the second and third Tests we had another practice game at a place called Vizag on the east coast. I looked at the hotel menu, saw the prawns and thought, 'Great!' I got through the night just fine but the next morning started to feel a little off. I was not listed to play in the practice game that day – but could not have anyway because while the team was warming up I was in the bathroom being as sick as I had ever been in my life.

The boys found it quite funny that I could hardly move and just lay there in the dressing room all day. But it started to become quite serious as I lost a lot of weight. Towards the end of the trip my teammates were calling me 'Skeletor' because my cheekbones were poking out of my face.

I did my best to rest and recover because I did not want to miss the third Test. Even though a bat had never felt so heavy in my hands, I managed to get out there and play my part in the final match of the tour, in Mumbai. I'm glad I did because we chased down a big score on the last day for a great win, a 'Test match' win for Australia.

Basics of travelling well

Getting sick on a tour is sometimes unavoidable. But it makes sense to take whatever steps possible to minimise the chance.

The last thing you want to do when you are travelling to play any sport – or for any purpose really – is add illness to your list of obstacles. It's hard enough trying to ensure you are in tip-top shape physically and mentally after a long flight and stepping into different conditions and a different culture.

The first steps to protecting your health and travelling well are the real basics, such as ensuring you have had the right vaccinations. The organisers of the tour, for instance Cricket Australia, a state or local association or club, should have this all worked out. But I believe that as an individual in charge of your own health and wellbeing it is every traveller's personal responsibility to be aware of what is required. You can do that with your own research, by speaking to your family doctor and asking questions of the team's associated medical staff.

Another basic thing I often consider whenever I travel is how best to deal with jet lag. What will the local time be when I arrive at my destination? What hours do I hope to sleep during the flight? Should I try to nap soon after I arrive? Would it be better to go for a walk or have a workout at the gym? These are important considerations because they can set you up for several days ahead. Cricketers often find themselves playing within hours of arriving, especially those turning up at a T20 tournament. Again, sometimes schedule changes are unavoidable and your best-laid plans can go out the window. But it's worthwhile at least preparing for how you anticipate events will unfold.

Travelling well to play sport is a lot about physical factors. But I found that many of the foundations to performing well on a tour are in the mind. There is plenty to enjoy about tours. But they can also be long and arduous, intense at times and downright unpleasant. Things go wrong. Players can be out of form and struggling. Tensions can be high. There can be personality clashes, selection frustrations, homesickness. All the kinds of pressures players usually endure tend to be magnified when you are a long way from home. Tours are often a big test of patience and discipline off the ground as much as on it.

One way I have noticed players keep grounded mentally is by being at peace with separating from what they have left behind. Everyone is excited to leave on a tour or join a tournament overseas but at some point pretty much everyone misses home.

It's important for everyone's state of mind to be empathetic to those who are holding the fort at home. For loved ones you said goodbye to, the time goes slowly and they really notice the loss. They are short a helper around the home and are just trying to get on with day-to-day duties. They are doing it tough while you are mostly having a great time – or, at least, it probably seems that way to them.

It's easy to disconnect from what is happening at home because you are focused on your cricket and all the action that is going on around you. There is also the luxury of falling back on the team environment in which there is almost always someone to chat to. Often the time zones make it challenging to be in touch with people at home, and the connections – both technological and emotional – can be fraught. However, in my experience I have found that maintaining a healthy link with family and close friends is important for the overall stability of your life and your cricket.

Another really big factor that I believe separates good tourists from bad is whether they can maintain a positive attitude and be a uniting force when the going gets tough. There is nothing worse than being trapped for days or weeks with a player who complains that the hotel is dirty, the shops never have what they want, the food is not what they thought it would be or whatever else. The influence of players with a poor attitude can be very negative on team spirit, whatever the team make-up or type of tournament or series that is being played.

By contrast, positive people on a tour can make themselves highly valuable team members. Even if they are not scoring runs or taking wickets they can have a big impact on the side's fortunes because they bring up the emotions of those around them.

Positive people on a tour will make suggestions, take initiative and look to be part of the team's activities. They will be keen to be involved in helping build the team culture. They will have a constructive influence on the people around them and in some cases make themselves indispensable just by their presence.

Staying positive on a cricket tour full of ups and downs is hard. But in the end you are travelling overseas, playing a game you love and being looked after by hosts who generally are trying their hardest to make your experience a good one. Maintaining a happy demeanour, keeping an open mind and a good spirit makes for a good teammate. These are what I consider the basics of travelling well.

Shantaram

Touring the cricket-playing countries offers great opportunities to develop as a cricketer but also as a person. You can find yourself in some amazing places and surprising situations beyond the cricketing environment. Finding time to get out and about can be difficult with all the training, playing and official functions. Certainly on an Australian team tour the days can be very busy. But there are occasional chances to get lost in the local culture, making for some unforgettable experiences.

One of my favourite travel tales while with the Australian team came on our visit to India in 2006 when three of us – Adam Gilchrist, me and I'm pretty sure it was Damien Martyn – were reading the novel *Shantaram* at the same time. *Shantaram* is an extraordinary novel based on the life of an Australian author, Gregory David Roberts, who is sent to prison in Victoria for armed robbery but forges a brazen escape and flees to India. He turns up in Mumbai where he hides among the slums and shantytowns believing he can blend in with the locals and steer clear of the authorities.

The book tells of how stories circulate through the slums that Lin – the main character – is a doctor. He goes along with it and soon people begin queuing up to be treated by him. Simultaneously, Lin starts to weave his way into the Mumbai underworld through which he is able to get supplies for his doctor day job.

Lin spends a few years living a fascinating, seedy and secret life before he falls in love with a German girl and follows her to Germany where he is eventually caught, deported back to Australia and returned to prison. Once his sentence is served he returns to settle in Mumbai. It is an amazing story that completely captivated us during that tour.

Throughout the book there are several mentions of a grubby old restaurant and bar called the Leopold Hotel where Lin does a lot of his dodgy dealing with underworld figures. He describes it as having dirty floors, plastic tables and chairs and a menagerie of weird characters loitering about.

One afternoon Gilly was walking about in Mumbai and spending some time away from the team when he came across Leopold's. He got really excited about it and when he got back to the hotel told us other readers to come down for a drink. We went down there, sat with our beers and thought, 'How good is this? We're actually at Leopold's!' Pretty soon the owner, who I think recognised Gilly, came over and joined us. Gilly started telling him that we were reading *Shantaram* and found it to be an amazing book.

'Oh, he lives very close by', the owner said. 'I'm going to call him and see if we can get him down for a visit.' We all just thought 'Woah!' Incredibly, about ten minutes later Gregory David Roberts was sitting at our table telling us about his new life in Mumbai. He looked just like Billy Birmingham, with long grey hair and deep wrinkles on a leathery face. He looked like he had seen plenty of action in his life. But he said he had cleaned up, no longer took drugs or drank and had a great memory for his experiences in the city, particularly at Leopold's, where he told us all about his dealings and the many shady figures he mingled with.

It was a fascinating conversation and a situation we were fortunate to stumble upon. There we were, three players from the Australian cricket team sitting in this dirty, dingy drug den hotel from a novel we were absorbed by, and within minutes we had the star of the book sitting there telling us extraordinary stories.

We are all ambassadors

I think most people when they travel consider themselves to be, to some extent, ambassadors for their country. I certainly do. I think we are all representatives and therefore have a responsibility that goes beyond enjoying ourselves and trying to win matches. I think there is a duty to behave well and act politely and respectfully. When you are part of an elite sporting team that idea is amplified because you are either literally wearing the national colours or being an Australian within a composite team and the eyes of the people you are visiting are fixed on you.

Not every player I have been associated with has shared my sentiment on this point. I have seen some players treat locals poorly or disrespected their customs and I have cringed at their behaviour. I think it says a lot about a person who acts like that. Behaving poorly as an Australian athlete overseas devalues the reputation of the team and Australia as a whole.

I think that sort of behaviour could be reduced if players spent a little more time making themselves aware of local customs and values before they travelled. The primary focus on a sporting tour is on athletic performance. Ultimately you are there to do a job. However, too often I have noticed we have gone to countries with an attitude of 'Righto, let's get this done and get out of here' instead of taking the time to understand and learn something about the places we are visiting. The people and their customs will, of course, be different – sometimes very different to what we are used to – but by embracing local cultures and customs, cuisine, ways of life and history, we represent ourselves, our teams and our country well and earn the respect of our hosts.

It's not just in the very different cultures, such as in the subcontinent, that I think Australians could improve their skills. Even in England I can recall instances when our cultural sensitivity and knowledge could have been better. We had the honour of meeting Queen Elizabeth II during the lunchbreak of a day's play at Lord's, but few of us had any idea how to address the Queen or what would be appropriate behaviour around her. Just moments before our meeting I was told we could call her Your Royal Highness or Your Majesty. Thank goodness for that! What a mess that moment could have become without that advice.

At the top level, I believe one of the reasons we are not as good at learning about local cultures as we could be is that we do not really have to. Everything is laid on a platter and life is very easy for us when we visit another place. In India, particularly, the people want to please and they want to be part of the cricket scene however they can. A cleaner might proudly go home to tell his family 'I washed Brett Lee's clothes today!' even if Brett might have been rude to him.

Not that I ever saw Brett treat someone badly when he was representing Australia. In fact, Brett, Adam Gilchrist and Matthew Hayden were among the most impressive players I toured with in terms of getting out and experiencing the local cultures and customs of the places they visited. Matthew liked to use local ingredients to cook up a storm when he was in a new place and often asked if he could get into the kitchens at our hotels and chat to the chefs. Adam was generally upbeat and took an interest in local customs and stories. Steve Waugh was great too. He would walk the streets and take great photos.

These guys were great travellers and it shone through in their positive approach to playing cricket.

With more and more intercultural crossover through T20 I believe players with better understanding and interest in other cultures will be better positioned to play open, positive cricket and be more highly valued as teammates. Just by being in a T20 team at the IPL or elsewhere there is the opportunity to speak to players from different backgrounds and learn about their ways of life. I have really enjoyed the chances in my time at the IPL to talk to Indians, Sri Lankans, South Africans and others and ask them about their countries and their lives. I have learned cultural aspects I did not know about, behaviour that is acceptable or not, ways of addressing people and topics that may be sensitive or celebrated. I have learned about domestic politics, culture and history.

For players yet to experience world competitions like the T20 tournaments, researching at least a little bit about the history and culture of places you are going to visit is a worthwhile step towards becoming a better person, a better teammate and a better tourist.

Around the cricket world

Since my first trip out of Australia on that under 19s tour to India way back in 1994 I have been fortunate to have travelled to India many times as well as around the rest of the cricket world and beyond. There may be only a fairly small number of full member International Cricket Council nations that Australian teams tour but they are very diverse and interesting and each comes with its own challenges.

India is a fabulous place to tour but it is intense. It is a big country, flights can be quite lengthy and there seems to be a lot of activity wherever you go. Cricketers are very highly thought of and there is little chance for time out if you are a recognisable face. The other really pressing thing about India for me was that, even years after that under 19s tour, it took me a long time to come to terms with the absolute beauty and opulence contrasted against such widespread poverty. I am not sure that even now it is something I can properly process.

Travelling anywhere in the subcontinent can be draining in good and bad ways. Sri Lanka is a bit less fanatical about cricket but it is still a hive of action for touring squads. It is a beautiful country, the food is really nice and the people are friendly. The grounds are a bit run-down but the authorities are making improvements as much as they can. The heat and humidity were always very difficult for me in Sri Lanka but it is a nice place to tour.

In the West Indies, somewhat like in India, you experience two opposite ends of the spectrum. There are so many incredibly beautiful beaches with warm, clear waters and spectacular destinations. One standout memory for me was going to St Vincent and heading to the top of a fort there and looking out over the deep blue ocean. It left me breathless, the beauty of it all. We had a team meeting up there and all I could think was that this was absolute paradise. But then you get back onto the main roads, which are full of holes and cracks, and you drive past dilapidated buildings. It is such a contrast from the most beautiful places you have ever seen to what are, essentially, Third World conditions. I remember feeling very sad for some of the locals when I heard about the many failed businesses, particularly traditional businesses like sugar cane farming. It is hard to fathom how life can be so hard in such a pristine place.

The quality of food and standard of hotels is ordinary in many parts of the Caribbean, the cricketing facilities are run-down, and travelling between the countries of the West Indies is a nightmare. Flights are almost always delayed or rescheduled, players have to get their own gear on and off flights and there are no lounges in which players can get away from the public glare. Travelling and playing cricket in the Caribbean can be hard going but it does provide for some magical moments.

South Africa is a fascinating place to tour and play cricket. Assuming you can handle the heavy diet of big steaks, starchy potatoes and big thick beers, there are many unique experiences to be enjoyed. We went to game reserves, sat up on Table Mountain in Cape Town and heard stories about Nelson Mandela on Robben Island. I remember letting my imagination run free, thinking about the incredible history of the country. Again, however, South Africa's great contrasts struck me. There is such pain and suffering going on for so many millions of people amid all the country's majesty.

Another big challenge to touring South Africa is that you are always a little more security conscious than you are in some other places. In my time travelling there, team management was always very strict with us about being outside the hotel, except in Cape Town. You always had to advise the team security officer if you wanted to go out and they would send a police escort with you. In local areas you would see guard dogs, huge fences around homes and barbed wiring. I found it a bit scary, especially when you would hear stories about former players being mugged. It is sad that this is part of the deal with touring South Africa because in general it is a nation of great spots, great people and good hard cricket.

England is very different again. For starters the travel is mostly by bus rather than air. The actual time spent getting from, say, Leeds to London can be similar to a lengthy flight in India or across the West Indies. But I always appreciated it because it meant escaping the airport check-in and security rigmarole and being able to stop whenever you wanted. It also was a way to travel without being around much of the public. English food can be quite heavy on the stomach, like South African, and the weather is, as we all know, questionable. But it is much more familiar to us Australians overall and therefore it's perhaps a little easier to feel comfortable there than some other places.

New Zealand is even more familiar than England. Travelling there for cricket is very casual and enjoyable. The security seems relaxed, the traffic is easy, there are good-quality hotels and food, nice grounds to play at and nice cool weather. There are generally smaller crowds of people to deal with, both at the cricket and around day-to-day activities, which gives a pleasant feeling – even if they are pretty hostile to us Aussies.

Feeling safe

With an increasing number of international players moving about between countries, playing in different tournaments for different teams, we might have to start rethinking the way cricketers are protected. I am no security expert, but I do know that the world today is very different from the one in which I started my career travelling around to play cricket.

At present, security at T20 tournaments, particularly the IPL, is extremely tight. Since the terrorist attack on the Taj Hotel in Mumbai in 2008 a presidential-style level of protection has been provided for all the players and teams, from the moment they arrive in India until the moment they leave. Sometimes it has felt to me as though the authorities have gone above and beyond the necessary measures for us to be guarded. It can feel daunting to be surrounded by armed police and military officers. But it is better to be safe than sorry.

Throughout the several weeks of an IPL tournament every bus trip is accompanied by an escort of two police cars and two armed officers on motorbikes. They whisk you through the traffic past hordes of people to the hotel. All vehicles entering the hotel while the players are staying are checked by bomb detectors and all people entering the building must go through bomb detection screening.

The team is kept together on one floor of the hotel, as much to stop approaches from match-fixers as for the players' physical protection. There are security personnel at the lifts and armed guards along the hallways twenty-four hours a day. Family members are allowed entry to the floor and any other visitors must be registered beforehand by the player inviting them.

Each team has a security liaison officer whom the players can ask for advice or approach with concerns. The officer ensures that protection standards are being met, that the players are in the right place at the right time, that the police and military personnel are doing their jobs properly and there are not let-ups or oversights. If you plan to go out on an unstructured trip, you must tell the liaison officer, who will either accompany you or organise an escort.

Security at the IPL is intense, to say the least. But I suppose it has to be. There are many different nationalities and religions in each team. At Chennai we had Catholics, Muslims and Hindus in our teams and players from numerous countries. India, at times, can be a hotbed. IPL 2 was staged in South Africa because the tournament was to coincide with the Indian national elections and cricket organisers were not satisfied enough security resources were available at a time when tensions could be heightened.

Such security arrangements, while seemingly over the top, give players a sense of safety. However, I think it is unwise to take for granted that there will never be a problem. I used to feel completely safe travelling around as part of the Australian team, and confident in the advice we received from the authorities. But with some shocking news in 2009 that sense of safety came crashing down and changed my view. I think it had a similar effect on many of the world's top cricketers.

Over the years Australian cricketers have had reason to feel confident that Cricket Australia (CA) undertook the best possible vigilance in the lead-up to tours. Before every tour, a representative from CA, the Australian Cricketers' Association and the Australian Federal Police would visit the destination. They would inspect each hotel, the grounds, the routes to the grounds and talk to local police and security agencies to find out what kind of support there would be. They would then collaboratively compile a report in which they would recommend whether the tour should go ahead. Particularly in recent years they have been very strict that a wide range of minimum standards must be in place before an Australian team went anywhere. I know of instances when our authorities refused to allow our team to tour until certain security arrangements were improved. However, even the most stringent standards are not foolproof.

In 2005 I was part of the Australia A tour to Pakistan. It was the aftermath of September 11, a touchy time especially in that part of the world. Yet there was no hint of discomfort within our group. The Australian High Commission had told us we had nothing to fear because in that region cricket was so loved that an attack on a team would be seen very negatively.

I took the High Commission's advice at face value and felt comfortable with it. But soon I had strong reason to wonder whether it was naive to be so accepting of such a conclusion. One night we went out for dinner in Old Lahore, returned to the hotel and woke to the news that a bomb had gone off a very short distance from where we had eaten. Understandably a lot of our squad was spooked.

Team management decided to hold a meeting of our group where we discussed whether we should stay on the tour or leave. It was an open and honest gathering in which people expressed views both ways. It was unlike any team meeting I had been involved in. People were listening intently and really considering all the information that was being presented. This was not about match tactics or training plans; it was about something much more serious than that.

The advice we received suggested that the attack had not been aimed at us. The device had been detonated in a marketplace at 9 am; it was a crude bomb and not the work of a suicide bomber or the result of a sophisticated plot. Our team manager relayed to us that Cricket Australia's directive was that we stay on the tour.

My belief was that while I agreed we should stay on the tour, I also felt that every one of us had to respect the views of the individuals in the group. If they felt their safety was in peril and did not feel comfortable staying on they should be allowed to leave.

I addressed the team at the meeting and expressed those views. However, I added two important points. First, I said, no one should make the decision to leave based on the fact that we had been in Pakistan for six weeks and they simply wanted to go home. It had been a long tour and we had all had enough. But I was adamant none of our players use this situation as an excuse or easy way to get an early ticket home.

Second, I said, everyone should be aware of the repercussions of leaving. For an Australia A team to pack up and abandon a tour would cause serious damage to cricket in Pakistan. It would not only make other nations less inclined to tour but also probably aid the cause of those seeking to disrupt normal life in the country. There were serious considerations to think about. Thankfully, we did stay on for the duration and everything was fine.

The foundation of my belief in staying on that tour of Pakistan had been the concept that – as in any of the subcontinental countries – there was no point attacking a cricket team as it would be a very unpopular move by any terrorist group. In 2009 that idea became baseless after the Sri Lankan team was attacked in a shocking and horrific incident in Lahore, when twelve gunmen set upon the team bus as they were en route to play on the third day of the second Test. Several local policemen and two civilians were killed and six members of the team were injured.

In the aftermath of that awful time I spoke to a number of Sri Lankan players who were on that bus – Murali, Ajantha Mendis, Thilan Samaraweera, Kumar Sangakkara, Mahela Jayawardene – and was stunned by how apparently unaffected they were by the whole thing despite the incredible descriptions they gave me of what had gone on. Each had vivid memories of the sound of the bullets hitting the metal of the bus and shattering the windows. They had all got on the floor, scared for their lives, and someone had screamed to the driver to step on the accelerator. They must have been horrifying moments.

When they got to the ground the wounded were attended to and most of the players got on their phones to call loved ones back home. It soon became clear what a miracle it was that more people were not killed: a rocket launcher had shot a missile just past the bus, a grenade thrown under the bus had failed to detonate and bullet holes riddled the vehicle's entire exterior. The difference between the team being at the heart of a complete disaster and emerging relatively unscathed was a matter of centimetres.

I am not sure what psychological effects the incident had on the players. Certainly some had serious questions about how and why such an incident was able to happen. Murali, particularly, was very concerned. He told me that the Sri Lanka team had travelled to the ground each day in convoy with the Pakistan team but on that day for some reason the Sri Lankans left at a slightly different time.

Who knows what conversations went on within the team and within the players' families. At least some of the partners and children must have wanted them to put an end to their travelling days. But, to a man, the Sri Lankans seemed unwilling to let the experience dampen their participation in the international world, and the fascinating and sometimes edgy life of the travelling cricketer. They considered themselves lucky, for sure, but did not alter course. They wanted to get on to the next destination, get ready for the next game and continue representing their country.

I remember after the initial shock of what had happened saying to myself, 'That's it. I am never going to play cricket in Pakistan again.' I, along with many others, felt from that moment that nothing could ever again be taken for granted when travelling to play. We would have to consider a lot more about the places we went, the situations we put ourselves in and how we went about our daily lives in different countries and regions.

It is purely hypothetical, as I have never had to deal with the after-effects of a terrifying experience such as the one the Sri Lankan team endured in 2009, but I believe I would have continued to play international cricket, as they each chose to, especially if I was early in my career. I have a wife and four kids at home and leaving them is never easy, especially when the risks of travelling the world to play cricket have never been more real.

However, the unique experiences, great moments – and the love for the game that many millions have in the countries we visit – always remained at the forefront of my mind.

SPIRIT AND CULTURE

One key ingredient

I have experienced two very strong and yet very different-feeling team cultures. The first was the Western Australia side I entered as a youngster, in which the culture was very much built around the idea of seniority. It was a team led by hardened professionals, including Tom Moody, Mike Veletta, Bruce Reid and Brendon Julian, who were highly successful cricketers and knew each other well personally and professionally.

Whenever a new pup came into the team the established players treated them harshly. They made you earn your stripes through extremely hard work and good performances before they would respect you or treat you as an equal. To be honest, as much as I enjoyed the challenging training, professionalism and discipline, I did not like being treated as a second-class citizen. But I had to accept that it was the environment in which I had to prove myself.

In a conversation with Moody some years later he told me that the reason he and the other senior guys had given the younger players such a hard initiation was that they wanted the new guys to know just how much of a privilege it was to play for WA. He said the seasoned members of the side were very protective of the team culture, wanted to make sure the WA cap was not taken for granted and ensure everyone knew there was plenty of work to do to become a respected member of a team representing our state.

The other environment I entered that had a strong culture was the Australian team. When I walked into that dressing room for the first time the feeling was almost the opposite of what it felt like early on at WA. There was still a core group of hardened professionals, including Ricky Ponting, Matthew Hayden, Justin Langer, Adam Gilchrist, Glenn McGrath and Shane Warne. But whatever fear I felt entering that environment dissipated almost immediately because of the warm welcome I received.

Unlike when I joined my state side, becoming part of the Australian team was an affirming experience. Straight away I was made to feel that I deserved to be there and was a valued and trusted member of the group. I felt much less pressure than I expected I would because the need to prove myself to my teammates was simply not there. It allowed me to quickly turn my attention to getting to know the team plans and what my role would be.

The fact that these sides had such different dynamics did not make one successful and the other mediocre. Both enjoyed great results around the times I joined them. WA was runner-up in the Sheffield Shield in 1995–96 and 1996–97 and won it the following two seasons, and the Australian team had a great run through 2006 and well beyond. In both cases a powerful team culture was a big contributing factor to success. But it did make me wonder what it says about culture that you can have two groups of cricketers with such a different atmosphere, yet both are able to use their culture to help them achieve highly.

I think it says there are different ways to build strong cultures within teams and different ways to express them. But when I more deeply compared those two sides I discovered there was one key ingredient they shared. Within each group was a rock-solid core of players who had been working together for the best part of a decade. They shared the element of time. Therefore, I believe, time is an essential factor in establishing a strong team culture.

In the WA and Australian sides there were players who had for many years been teammates, travelled together, trained and prepared together and socialised together. They had been through all sorts of ups and downs as a group. Shared experiences over years meant that robust relationships had been developed, built around an enormous amount of trust and respect. It enabled the squads to hold open and honest conversations about all subjects, good or bad. Healthy communication lines meant everyone was familiar with their individual roles and knew the team's plans and methods. Away from the game, too, respect and trust were valuable aspects of the team culture as they allowed the players to relax in each other's company, confide in each other and celebrate wins together.

Turnover

As time is such a crucial part of the puzzle, it's little surprise that the Australian team culture came under pressure when several of the old guard began retiring. After the retirement of Shane Warne, Glenn McGrath and Justin Langer in 2007, Adam Gilchrist in 2008 and Matthew Hayden in 2009, all of a sudden some of the central figures in a culture that seemed impenetrable were no longer there and had been replaced by nearly half a team of new players. It changed the feeling in the side a lot and I think there are plenty of lessons to be learned from what happened in the following years.

One large impediment to maintaining some link to the strength of the previous team culture was that many of the players who were brought into the side after the big retirements were either very young, perceived as not having worked hard enough to earn a place in the Test team, or both. Particularly around 2010 and 2011 there was a big push for really young players to be picked. The older guys tended to feel let down by that policy. They felt there were experienced players who had been working incredibly hard for many years at first-class level who deserved to be in the side more than some of those who were given a go.

I admit there were times I looked at some guys in the dressing room and questioned whether they had done enough to deserve an opportunity to play for Australia. I would see someone like Ed Cowan and feel comfortable with him as a teammate, as he had consistently dominated at first-class level. More recently, Chris Rogers became another example of someone who worked tirelessly and scored thousands of runs before being selected. It was much easier to feel respect for Ed and Chris than some others, who seemed to be selected more on potential than a proven record.

I feel that picking guys based on their potential rather than their achievements developed a soft culture in the team. It devalued the honour of earning a baggy green, which concerned a number of the senior players in the team and outside it. The policy showed cricketers all over the country – and the public too – that all a young player had to do was show potential and they were in with a real chance of becoming one of the select few to play Test cricket for Australia.

As well as a soft culture, picking young inexperienced players developed a losing culture, as these guys were simply not ready or up to the task of playing consistent hard cricket at the very top level. It seemed to me there was an acceptance that personnel turnover meant we were going to lose games. It was not good for anyone's confidence or morale and put extra pressure on the senior guys, who had to cover for the inexperience and inadequate skills of the younger blokes. I certainly felt extra responsibility around that time. There is enough pressure already in international cricket, let alone having more added on. Overall I felt that none of the effects of overlooking hardened and long-serving Sheffield Shield players and selecting potential future stars helped maintain or develop our team culture.

The problem became compounded by the fact that the new arrivals were not even given the chance to establish themselves. The policy was challenging enough as it was, but maybe if the selectors had stuck with a new group for, say, two years, the players could have gained a decent feel for the team and helped rebuild the culture or taken it in a new and positive direction.

They might have become more comfortable in meetings, more involved in decision-making on and off the field and felt more ownership within the side. But the selectors did not give them that opportunity.

A number of players came into the side for a handful of games and if they did not perform well they were dropped. There was so much chopping and changing that team unity and spirit were never given a chance to develop. Suddenly we had to get to know new people all the time, tour with them, try to learn about them, make them feel welcomed and comfortable only for them to be axed. Someone else would come in and we would have to start again.

There is nothing wrong with picking a young player to join a team of pros. Sometimes a youthful influence can invigorate a culture with new energy. It can give the youngster a chance to soak up the team ethos so he can pass it on down the track. But bringing in several young players within a short time risks creating a clash of philosophies and behaviours that can become almost impossible to manage. It becomes much harder again when players are coming in and out of the side so often.

The crossover of generations in the Australian team was quite profound at stages after the retirements of some of the great players who were in the team that I joined. It led to some problems as the younger players rejected suggestions, directions and even the leadership of the older players. Some of the seasoned members of the side were genuinely stunned at how differently the Gen Y guys viewed the game and their place within the team framework. None of us really knew how to deal with the issues.

Continuity

Assuming new players are introduced methodically, have the right personalities and a positive attitude, team culture can be passed down from one generation to another without too much difficulty. The experienced guys must be willing to promote it and the young guys must be willing to listen and learn. The incumbents set the standards and the new players have the opportunity over time to then develop their own ideas, maybe add something and eventually, when they feel ready, constructively question aspects of the culture and suggest ways they might be improved.

I am loath to say anything negative about the leaders within the group around the time the Australian team went through its big changeover of players, as it was a very difficult situation that no one was prepared for. But we might have taken a more proactive approach to protecting what we had and educated the new arrivals about what kind of culture existed and what aspects of it we wanted to keep and build upon.

I remember seeing one of the more established team members speak really poorly to one of the newer guys and no one said anything. I wish, in hindsight, one of the senior guys – me, Ricky or Michael, perhaps – had pulled him aside and said something like 'Please don't do that. That is not acceptable in our team culture.' We let things drift a bit instead of nipping incidents like that in the bud and setting more clearly defined parameters. We could have been more resolute about what we stood for as a team and made sure that every single member of the team knew exactly what that was.

One problem might have been that we never actually worked together to clearly define what our team culture consisted of.

In my early days in the Australian side the senior players told me about a document that was produced when Steve Waugh was captain that outlined what the team stood for, what the team was all about and what values it held. Just the fact that the document existed made guys think about culture as an essential part of our structure. That sort of blueprint or guide-line was never around later on when the younger guys were coming in and out of the team. It might have been beneficial in such circumstances.

Culture was never really talked about with regards to the new players entering the side after the big retirements. They would attend a short induction meeting where they would be told to be punctual, wear the right clothes and so on, but there was never a discussion about the team's philosophies or ways of going about its business. It must have been hard for those young players to suddenly find themselves playing cricket for their country and also having to try to work out for themselves what kind of a culture they were expected to fit into.

The lack of discussion might have been due to the increased obligations we all faced. By that time there were many more commitments such as media, more training, more games and more sponsorship expectations than when I had first joined the Australian team. The days always seemed to be filled up and the last thing you wanted to do at the end of it all was talk about values and culture. However, the price of bypassing discussion about what we stood for and what we were about was a missed opportunity to avoid the problems that arose later. We needed to work at our culture, contribute to it, think about it and not just leave it to filter through whoever might be in the dressing room at the time.

Helping teammates settle in

Almost always a new player will want to just concentrate on their immediate task, which is to play well enough to stay in the team. For an initial period they will mostly stay quiet and keep their head down rather than engage with what is going on around them. It takes time to move to the next level of confidence and engagement and I believe senior players need to be sensitive to that.

After reflecting on the difference I felt entering the WA and Australian teams, I felt it important to try to make the new guys feel welcome and valued, whether or not I agreed with their selection. I liked the way Adam Gilchrist had always been very big on making sure new arrivals felt comfortable, emphasising particularly the value of getting to know the whole person rather than just the cricketer. Often he would sit a new player down and say, 'Tell us five things about you that we don't know.' It was a small way to start building trust and provide a way for people to bond. 'Oh, you said your sister's a champion skier? I'm interested in skiing', and a conversation would be started.

Around the time that we had a lot of changeover, Justin Langer, our batting coach, implemented a mentor system, which I think was a positive move. It involved joining up a senior player with a new one and gave the new guy someone in a semi-formal sense that he could bounce ideas off or ask questions of. Often the pair would grab lunch together or a coffee and just be buddies.

I volunteered to be Nathan Lyon's mentor after he joined the team for the Test tour of Sri Lanka in 2011 and consequently we built up a good relationship over a couple of years. I really enjoyed getting to know Nathan and passing on some of my knowledge and experience of playing international cricket. I found him to be a good bloke; I liked the way he looked at the world and the way he approached his cricket. Nathan proved to be down to earth and always looking for ways to contribute to the team. I really wanted him to succeed for himself and our team and did what I could to help.

Nathan eventually found his feet in the side and is enjoying a fine Test career. But there are others I think we could have done a better job of helping to settle in. One example was Cameron White, one of the most talented cricketers you could ever hope to have as a teammate but someone who seemed to find it hard to feel at ease as an international cricketer.

The reason I raise Cameron as an example is that I remember him saying in the press, after he had played quite a few international one-dayers, that he felt he was still trying to impress his teammates. I felt very disappointed by that comment, not because of anything Cam did wrong but because it said to me that we as a team had let him down. It told us that we had a player in our side who felt so alienated from the rest of us that he felt he needed to prove himself time and again. It told us there was a problem with our culture.

What was at issue was not whether Cameron was welcome in the team or whether he was a good enough player. On both counts everything was fine. He was good around the team environment, trained hard and had a positive attitude. I think most if not all the guys felt glad to have him in the side. The problem was that he did not feel that appreciation. The fact that we had a player in our side who felt uncomfortable was a blight on our team. It was our duty to act on that.

I certainly could have taken more of an active role in helping Cameron. I had spoken to him and told him what Warney had told me – you deserve your place, play your natural game, we are glad to have you here – but maybe he needed more than that. Maybe he needed to hear it from other teammates too. Maybe he needed to hear something else altogether. Perhaps I could have gone to the team leadership and discussed how we might better integrate Cam. Maybe we could have looked at team-building exercises, linked him up with different players or just created a forum for him to speak openly about what he was going through.

It's not anyone's right to say how a player should or should not feel. The fact is that Cameron felt a particular way and we should have been better at sorting out the problem for the benefit of Cam and the team as a whole. If I had my time again I would do more to help him than I did. He had the courage to speak up in public about his struggles to feel part of the team and it should have been a wake-up call for all of us. It also should have been an alert that there were possibly other players who felt the same way but suffered in silence.

Captaincy

Senior players lead team culture and there are none more senior in a cricket team than the captain and vice-captain. It would be wrong to examine the lessons learned from the team's difficult period of transition without taking a look at what happened at the top.

In previous years the balance between the captain and vice-captain seemed to work well. Allan Border was known as a very headstrong character but his understudy, Geoff Marsh, seemed very stable. He kept things ticking along and was careful not to rock the boat too much. Marsh showed loyalty and support for his captain throughout his tenure. It appeared to work well even if it did not inspire great changes or developments in the way the team went about its processes.

Adam Gilchrist was a great vice-captain. He was loyal but also had the self-confidence and tact to speak up and offer suggestions. Adam would raise his criticisms and suggestions in a constructive way, discussing things thoughtfully and positively and always searching for workable outcomes. Neither Marsh nor Gilchrist became captains. However, Michael Clarke was identified quite early as being the successor to Ricky Ponting and was groomed for the role while he was still the deputy.

Back then we all knew that Michael had a great feel for tactics, an exemplary work ethic and was becoming a long-serving member of the side. He seemed an obvious choice to take over and Ricky wanted to play his part by helping Michael learn as much about the job as possible. The challenge, as I saw it, was that Ricky and Michael were from different cricketing generations and at either ends of the spectrum on how they saw the game.

When it became apparent that Ricky was getting closer to retirement there were times on the field when Michael would run over to Ricky and put forward his opinions. Sometimes it led to tension between them. However, the concept was right, as it showed that Michael was thinking about the game and it was useful for the captain to hear a variety of ideas.

Often a captain can feel quite isolated when he is making all the decisions hour after hour. Having input from those around him, whether they are experienced players or younger players, can open up possibilities the skipper might not have considered. For a younger player, particularly, to be heard and considered has the potential to raise his confidence. The key, however, is that it is the captain's duty to make the final call and, whatever he decides, every member of the team has the responsibility to be loyal and back their skipper.

A healthy pattern of information sharing during play is an example of good culture at work. Everyone can provide input and the captain and vice-captain set the example. However, when a link falls down within this structure, problems can arise. The price can be the team pulling in different directions, confidence issues, especially among younger players, and cliques being formed in which some team members back one authority over another.

Like challenging the captain on the field, providing alternative views in team meetings can be beneficial. It was quite commonplace in the Australian teams I had been a part of. When I joined the side there was a group of tough and seasoned players who had big egos and knew they were going to be selected pretty much no matter what. They were certainly not afraid to speak their minds. Guys like Matthew Hayden had no problem taking it up to the coach or the captain. Ricky was very strong-willed too and rarely gave an inch when he felt strongly about something.

Personality clashes and disagreements occurred in team meetings, but the thing that made it work was that they were always addressed on the spot. Dirty laundry was never left to fester. It was always sorted through in the moment and a conclusion was reached. Everyone would feel pleased the issues were done and dusted and we could all get on with our job of preparing well and playing well.

I think we were lucky to have Gilchrist, who really was a master at mediating tension. He would calm everyone down and get to the heart of the problem. Maybe if he had been around later on, the team culture would not have been compromised by the big personalities and clashes they had. Gilchrist was a vital figure in maintaining team harmony during Ricky's early leadership. But when Ricky was replaced by another very headstrong leader in Michael, there was no Gilly around to act as an arbitrator to resolve conflict.

The unofficial role of mediator could have been mine to fill. I was a player with a lot of experience, reasonably secure in the side at that time and felt I was viewed by my teammates as quite well balanced. However, conditions became very unusual. Not only was the team going through transition, but Michael also became a selector.

It was a challenging time because with Michael having such a close relationship with CA through his dual roles, it made it difficult for the players to feel comfortable challenging his ideas or directions either on or off the field. The worry for the players was that their opinions could jeopardise their spot in the team. The result was that constructive ideas were suppressed and players stayed in their shells. Everyone seemed to look inwards instead of outwards and kept grievances to themselves. We were all working very hard but there was little open conversation. Instead of looking at ways to contribute, it became about just trying to not put a foot wrong. It was not conducive to a great team culture.

There were times I wanted to discuss issues with Michael – around the direction of the team, ways we could build our unity, our spirit, ways we could approach different opponents we were going to face, all sorts of subjects – but I did not feel completely safe to bring them up. I knew Michael wanted to do things his way, as pretty much all captains do. But with the title of selector added to his role, I was worried – rightly or wrongly – that if I caused anything that could be interpreted as a stir I could be out the door.

Even looking back now it is hard to know what approach would have been best in those circumstances. If I'd been more confident in some ways I might have had the courage to speak up, aired my feelings and ideas and done more to help strengthen our culture at that time. For what it's worth, my form throughout that testing period was probably better than it had ever been. However, playing cricket driven by fear – and contributing little more to the team than just runs – was never the way I wanted to play my cricket.

Skills for life

The skills our team needed to employ to get out of our predicament are the kinds of skills that can be applied to maintaining a strong culture within a family, among friends, in intimate relationships and in business. Generally, a good work ethic, open and honest communication, clear plans, loyalty, trust and the ability to celebrate the good times with each other transcend across different lifestyles and form the foundation of good links between people. When disputes arise, just like in a team, people need to be patient and work effectively and diligently together to achieve a positive outcome.

From my experience in life and in cricket I have found that when high-pressure situations arise it's important to try to get a handle on the personalities involved so as to work out the best way to convey constructive points and ideas. Getting angry or aggressive rarely works out well in the end. Finding a quiet setting away from the team, away from the family, away from your co-workers or whomever, and expressing your thoughts positively and respectfully is the way to go. Ask if the other person agrees and listen to their thoughts without judgement.

These are skills I did not have when I was playing for Australia. I wish I did. I have thought about them more as I have become older and reflected on the way I saw my fellow cricketers address cultural problems within teams, helping people settle in, making people feel included and valuable, dealing with conflict – all sorts of situations that arose. There will always be disagreements and problems to solve and there are right and wrong ways to address them.

It is surprising to me that more effort is not invested in helping athletes become stronger in these vital skills. Some people, like Adam Gilchrist, have a natural knack for getting the balance right between being constructively assertive and being sensitive to people's personalities and situations. But I believe they are also skills that can be taught. Athletes who can gain a scientific understanding of communication and conflict resolution could potentially make themselves more valuable to their teams. Had we had more players with those skills in our teams over recent years it might have helped us better overcome some of the obstacles we experienced.

Twenty20 team culture

We have seen how vital time is as a factor in building a good team culture. Test and One Day International (ODI) teams often have time on their side as there are generally a number of long-serving players who can drive team values and spirit and teach the new guys. It's so important for those teams too because players go on long tours together, living in each other's pockets, and it is essential in those environments to have trust, respect and strong relationships.

For the IPL and Big Bash League (BBL), with players coming from across the world to play a fast-paced competition before going their separate ways, there is no time to establish a real sense of belonging, trust and respect. There might be some chance of building a decent team culture if players stayed just with one club year after year. But the constant movement between franchises eliminates even that possibility. The question I have considered lately is, does it really matter?

With Test and fifty-over teams I think the way a player fits into the team culture needs to be very seriously taken into account. Justin Langer often talks about 'character over cover drives' and I agree with him wholeheartedly. I wanted every player in my teams to be good at what they did. However, if one player was not quite as good as the next guy but was of good character, well respected and team-minded, I would take him over the one who offered nothing beyond scoring runs or taking wickets.

I used to think the same of T20 teams. Increasingly, though, I am doubting that. I am beginning to think of T20 as a different beast entirely. There are some players around who are not regarded as great team men or great characters and don't offer much in terms of building team culture. Yet they have the capacity to single-handedly win games for you. Do you want that sort of player on your side to hopefully blast a couple of wins for you during a six-week tournament? Or do you want someone who will put the team first, contribute in team meetings, train hard and set standards? It's a challenging question but the answer might become more apparent in years to come.

FAIR PLAY

Fair what?

The team walks out onto the ground together and they pause about halfway out to the middle. They link arms and the captain begins to deliver a big rev-up speech. You see it all the time these days in every form of cricket and, for that matter, most team sports. It probably looks impressive on television and for people in the crowd. The thing is, after you have played for long enough those kinds of moments become virtually meaningless. The same sorts of phrases are said every time and often you get the sense it's just a bit of filler or part of the public theatre.

I remember in a lot of those moments feeling as though my mental and physical preparation was done, I knew what I had ahead of me and was ready. I did not need – especially just moments before the start of play – someone telling me how hard we had to play, how sharp we had to be or how much this game meant. If the captain or leading player had to deliver a last-minute rev-up I hoped he would be able to come up with a new message that could add something useful as we were about to undertake our task.

That moment came during an IPL match I played for Chennai against arch rivals Bangalore in 2012. It was delivered by that man again, MS Dhoni. The match was in front of a rocking Chennai crowd. The noise was unbelievable and the tension enormous. We walked out onto the ground to massive cheers and an expectation to win. Amid all the pressure, sure enough, we were summoned together for the usual pre-match pump-up speech that no one really cared about.

To my complete surprise Dhoni began with: 'Boys, at the moment we are on top of the competition's fair play award. It is very important that we win the fair play award so let's work towards that.' He went on: 'If you miss a ball and the umpire gives you out you must not show any dissent towards the umpire, you must walk away.' Also he said, if the bowler has a batsman plumb LBW and the umpire says not out, 'There is no need to show you are upset. We must get our full points for the fair play award.' I thought, 'Wow! That was not what I was expecting!'

Dhoni's fair play chat was a bolt out of the blue. But knowing MS it was probably a bit of calculated brilliance aimed at trying to lighten everyone's mood and diffuse the strain of the moment. He probably sensed that some of the guys in the side were a bit uptight and we might make a better start to the game if we were a little more relaxed. Still, there were certainly a few quizzical looks around the group, more so from the foreign players than the Indian players, who would hang off every word the captain said.

Why did we think MS's words were peculiar? Put simply it was because fair play awards are treated as a joke by just about all top cricketers. Most players spend no time thinking about them. In the moments before, during and after a game, players rarely concern themselves with how their conduct will affect the way their team is perceived. Their only aim is to be on top of their game, play their best cricket and win. In the heat of battle, added responsibilities or distractions are the last thing you want – and fair play is viewed by most players as a distraction from the immediate task.

The irony is I think most players would tell you they see themselves as custodians of the game who have a responsibility to play cricket in the right manner and spirit. They would accept that they have a role to play in upholding the game's traditions and in ensuring parents see cricket as a good sport for their children to be involved in. They want cricket to be perceived as a sport of integrity through which youngsters can learn good values and morals. Elite cricketers want their sport to be held in high regard.

The challenge is that balancing the ideals of fair play with being successful in modern cricket is extremely difficult. Cricket at the top level is unbelievably tense and cutthroat these days. There is a huge demand for results, big money is invested and livelihoods are on the line. Cricket is a business that is much more heavily focused on winning than even just a few years ago. The notion of fair play is easily lost amid such hypercompetitiveness.

While we wish for the game to be played fairly and in good spirit, in such a pressurised environment players often overstep the line, as we regularly see. Cricket at any level is an emotional game, but it's especially so when you're playing for your country or a multimillion-dollar franchise and your career. Things bubble over in the contest and mistakes are made. I do not think there are many players who can say they have never overstepped the mark of what is generally viewed as acceptable behaviour, no matter how committed they are to playing the game 'the right way'.

Evolution of fair play

Fair play has gone through a number of phases over the years, but there are a few key moments and factors that have brought us to the tricky point we are at now. In the early days fair play was seen as the foundation of cricket. The sport was amateur, social and famously referred to as 'the gentleman's game'. Players would be clapped on and off the ground by opponents, cordiality prevailed and stories of virtuous behaviour had as much or even more value than athletic achievements. Rivalries and competitiveness existed but the concept of how you conducted yourself as an individual and as a team overarched the entire pursuit.

Then came Bodyline in 1932, which I would say was the first real test of cricket's gentlemanly principles. It sparked heated discussion about what the game's spirit actually meant. It tested the boundaries of what had been commonly held beliefs and caused the public and cricket authorities to confront the idea of winning at all costs versus protecting those early concepts of the game as a noble and dignified endeavour. I think the most significant outcome of the Bodyline series was that the governing body at the time, the Marylebone Cricket Club (MCC), changed the laws of the game to protect the nature of the way it was played, a landmark moment that we have seen happen many times since. Bodyline was a crucial event in the evolution of cricket's relationship with the concept of fair play.

Throughout the 1950s and 1960s there was a regression from the approach of winning at all costs and 'the gentleman's game' made a resurgence. On-field behaviour was mostly placid and mellow and many would argue that the game became quite boring and one-dimensional as a result. Those circumstances provided the perfect conditions for the Packer era, which unleashed a new type of cricket and new type of cricketer in the 1970s. The limited-overs revolution marked the beginning of a brash competitiveness and character personified in Australia by players such as Dennis Lillee, Doug Walters and the Chappell brothers. That tradition developed throughout the 1980s with the likes of Allan Border in Australia, Viv Richards and his great West Indies side, and Ian Botham in England. By the time I started playing for WA in 1994, first-class cricket had become a ruthlessly competitive environment and no place for the faint-hearted.

My memory of my early days in the Sheffield Shield was that NSW, South Australia and Queensland were vicious sledgers. Victoria had chirpers such as Dean Jones, who would be at you from the moment you came to the crease until you were well on your way back to the rooms. Queensland and South Australia played in the final in 1994–95 and were full of real hard nuts, including Darren Lehmann, Jamie Siddons and James Brayshaw at the Redbacks and Trevor Barsby, Stuart Law and Border at the Bulls. Western Australia was in on the act with Damien Martyn, Justin Langer, Brendon Julian and others pressing every button they could to gain their team an advantage.

Back in those days plenty was said in the middle that would not be acceptable now. I remember a game against South Australia when I copped it so badly from Lehmann, Siddons and Brayshaw – not to mention Greg Blewett, Tim May and Tim Nielsen – that our captain, Tom Moody, went into their dressing room after play and said, 'I'm all for a bit of chat but you guys have gone too far.' Tom was no shrinking violet. For him to do that, well, you can imagine some of the things that had been said.

In those days you could get away with all sorts of nasty behaviour without any real repercussions. There were no stump microphones, far fewer cameras around the ground and very little public or media scrutiny of on-field behaviour. If a complaint was made it was the umpire's word against a player's. It rarely happened anyway because generally the umpires were pretty liberal with letting players get away with poor behaviour – though they drew the line at spitting. It sounds almost impossible to believe spitting actually happened out in the middle, but believe me it did. Many players would agree, I think, that player conduct in those days sometimes got a bit out of control.

Since then, in the time that I have been playing, I have felt a noticeable shift back towards stricter definitions of fair play and more importance being placed on the way the game is perceived by fans and the general community. In-game technology has shone a spotlight on the way players behave and led to public debates about what is or is not acceptable. Sledging has been a big point of contention, particularly in Australia, where the national team's conduct has come under heavy scrutiny at times and bigger penalties for unsavoury conduct have been introduced. Many of the directives towards the Australian cricket team have come from Cricket Australia, which knows that the sporting landscape is more competitive than ever and the game's image is important to protect so as to continue drawing new participants, supporters and sponsors.

There is no doubt the market is highly competitive. But I think in some ways that the desire to move back towards a strong spirit of cricket is a legacy of the game's earliest days. The concept of the gentlemen's game is largely ingrained in the sport. It's part of the fabric of cricket. Despite all the changes and advancements of recent times, the hypercompetitiveness, business interests, sponsorships and so on, cricket is still, at heart, for better or worse, a very conservative and antiquated game.

The fact that cricket's foundation was built on the notion of 'the gentlemen's game' poses challenges in the modern environment. But it also provides cricket with a competitive advantage. There are very few other sports that can claim to be founded on etiquette and integrity. It is a point of difference administrators are rightly keen to protect and exploit. However, they also want to provide for supporters at the other end of the scale, who like to see the Australian team go hard and compete aggressively. These competing forces make for an interesting starting point for discussion on the importance and role of fair play in cricket.

The many shades of fair play

One of the most difficult aspects of assessing fair play is that the concept itself is open to individual judgement. It's about moral values, which differ from person to person. Within teams there are numerous personalities, different opinions and ways of seeing the world. No team can genuinely hold one united position on what is exactly 'the right spirit' with which to play the game. Those splits become magnified between nations, where cultural influences come into play. What one national cricket team feels is fair and dignified behaviour another might not. The same applies to fans.

Interpreting fair play is at the centre of the debate. These days cricket has many rules governing the topic. Yet there are still many areas of the game left open to interpretation. For instance, there is an age-old unspoken rule that if a fielder throws at the stumps and it hits the batsman and deflects away, the batting pair should not take advantage and take more runs. But what if that situation arises in a World Cup final? What if your country needs two runs to win, you hustle a quick single, the fielder throws, it deflects off your pads and goes away for another possible run? You suddenly have the chance to seal the World Cup for your country. Would you take the run? The rules say you can. Some people would back you but many others would say it's not the right thing to do.

My immediate feeling is that I would take the run. I am competitive, I love Australia and I would want us to win the World Cup. As long as the rules say it's OK, it's fine by me. But the more I think about it the more reason for doubt comes into my mind. Maybe taking that run would stain my reputation forever. 'Mike Hussey, the bloke who took that run in the World Cup final when he shouldn't have.' Then again, what if I didn't take it? Maybe I would be stained as the guy who cost Australia the World Cup because he was too concerned about fair play. Talk about being stuck between a rock and a hard place! To be able to make a life-changing judgement in an instant in a World Cup final about whether to take that extra run is a very heavy burden for any cricketer to bear. It shows how morally loaded the concept of fair play can be. It shows that it's impossible to please everyone when making such decisions.

It's not just at the top level that judgements about 'the right spirit' have to be made. What happens when the fourth-grade team you are playing for needs two runs to win and the same thing happens? These guys have been out there all day battling away in the heat among the flies, playing the best they can to try to win the match for their club and their mates. It does not matter if there are two men and a dog watching the play, because in that moment, in the thick of the contest, nothing matters more to those players than the game they are invested in. It is their Test match, their World Cup, and the same individual judgements about fair play need to be made.

Players at all levels of the game face conundrums about fair play, but it's at the top level that these decisions can reverberate and make a huge impact across nations. Representative teams have an enormous responsibility. Yet the different interpretations and values held by people about fair play have made it challenging for the Australian team especially to play in a way it considers to be typically Australian.

In my time in the national team we did genuinely care about the way we played with regard to setting a good example and representing our country with dignity and class. But we were often questioned and criticised about our approach and behaviour, sometimes from within Australia and sometimes from outside. Many people felt that at times we did not play in the right spirit and that our behaviour was not as good as it could have been. Whenever these debates came up our response – which was 100 per cent honest – was that we believed we played the game aggressively and would make no apologies for that. But we also believed we played the game fairly. I always felt that, in comparison with ball tampering and spot fixing, we upheld the spirit of the game pretty well.

Australian cricket provided plenty of examples of what I would consider fair play that are rarely considered as such when debates arise. I always thought of fair play as much more than being considerate of opponents or not purposely scuffing up the pitch. I saw it as being about things like partnerships within a team. If a guy is bowling well at one end, supporting him at the other end and acknowledging his contribution is an example of fair play. In batting, a player might tell his mate that he is struggling against a particular bowler and the other batsman will take more of the heat at one end. That's fair play. I remember at the WACA Ricky Ponting was struggling against Ishant Sharma in a match. I was at the other end and backing up so far so I could get on strike and shield Ricky until he could gather himself. There is a lot going on within good teams that I consider examples of what the spirit of cricket is about. But many of them are rarely considered within the discussion.

Having said that, the Australian team knew we sometimes sailed close to the wind and no doubt there were times when players crossed the line of what was acceptable. But Ricky never tried to curb anyone's behaviour. Perhaps the reason he took that approach was that everyone was aware of the rules. Each individual knew that if he overstepped the mark there would be consequences such as suspensions and fines. I viewed the members of our team as being like any member of society – everyone knows that robbing a bank is wrong and will result in penalties but it's not something you need to remind every individual each time they walk into a bank. Responsibility for behaviour in the Australian team belonged with the individual.

Everyone in the team accepted there were repercussions for stepping over the line and the fact that those repercussions could affect the team made them work quite effectively. Ricky might never have made a point about individuals' conduct but he did regularly point out that by being suspended you would be letting the team down. He reminded everyone that they were important to the team's stability and performance and by getting rubbed out for a match or two the side would be under unnecessary strain.

The walker

Rules governing aspects of on-field conduct are clear-cut. But there is the potential for arguments or splits to occur within sides when people in the group disagree on interpretations of the spirit of the game. I do not recall an Australian player putting his understanding of fair play above the team's collective desire for results. But Adam Gilchrist probably came closest, and I think a lot of people to this day remain unsure about how they feel regarding some of the decisions Gilchrist made around fair play, especially his stance on 'walking'.

I was always taught by my dad that 'the man in white is always right'. What Dad meant was it is the job of the umpire to make decisions. If he makes a decision you do not agree with or is simply wrong you put your bat under your arm, show no dissent and walk off (just like MS Dhoni said to do that day at Chennai). But it also meant that if you did edge one and the umpire gave you not out you were entitled to take that lucky break and carry on batting. I took that lesson right through my career. What it boiled down to was that you had to cop the good decisions with the bad.

Gilchrist thought differently. If he knew he hit the ball and was caught out, regardless of the umpire's judgement, he decided the right thing to do was to end his innings. It was obviously something he felt very strongly about because he did it in the semifinal of the World Cup against Sri Lanka in 2003. Attempting a sweep shot off Aravinda de Silva, Adam got an edge onto his pads, the ball flew up and was caught by wicketkeeper Kumar Sangakkara. The Sri Lankans appealed and umpire Rudi Koertzen said 'not out', but Gilly turned around and headed for the pavilion. It was an extraordinary moment and some of our players thought it was a bit over the top for him to make that call in such a massive game. Thankfully, we went on to win and then beat India in the final.

It's easy to think of someone who 'gives up their wicket' like that as lacking in competitive spirit. But in this case nothing could be further from the truth. I played for many years with Adam and I can tell you he was fiercely competitive. Apart from his incredible feats with the bat, which destroyed opposition teams and won so many games for Australia, behind the stumps he would go hard at batsmen and get right in their ear if he felt it would give us an edge. He hated losing as much as anyone and pushed the rules to the limit in many respects. But it was the walking debate that set him apart.

I think Adam got to a point in his career where he began to feel there were more important things in the game than winning. It was not about forging a unique brand or building his reputation, it was about his view on the values of cricket and the values of sportsmanship contrasted against the 'win at all costs' mentality that was starting to hold much more sway around that time.

Really, Adam's walking should not have been such a big deal. The rules of the game are pretty straightforward: if you hit the ball with your bat and it is caught by an opponent, you are out. The thing that made Adam different was that no one else would walk in those instances. Everyone else, including me, would wait for the umpire to decide their fate and take the lucky break if it worked out that way.

As frustrating as it could be as a teammate – and notwithstanding the fact that he had to walk, too, when he was incorrectly given out – I came to admire my teammate for his stance. It was not because I felt he was right or wrong. It was simply that he was an immensely talented cricketer playing on the biggest stage, yet he was willing to follow his true belief on a very important issue. Gilly played cricket with great integrity and was almost unanimously respected around the world for it. It's hard to fault him for his approach on the question of walking.

The (dark) art of sledging

To most Australians, from what I have gathered over the years, fair play does not preclude you from having a few words to your opponent in the heat of battle. Australians like being represented by aggressive, hard-nosed competitors who rise to their best in the toughest moments. They have a great knowledge of the game and understand that Test cricket is a test of strength, endurance and character. They realise that talking to a batsman while he is at the crease can be an effective tool in putting him off his game by interrupting his concentration. Some may call it sledging, others gamesmanship. Whatever it's called, as long as it's not vilifying, it's within the rules and I do not have a problem with it.

I was never much good at using words to put a batsman off. The first guy I sledged made 150 and the second made 200, and that was about the end of my experimenting with that part of the game. But using psychological tactics was something our teams did quite a lot of study on, especially during the John Buchanan coaching era, when we looked into personality types and the best ways to use them to our advantage. Phil Jauncey, a performance psychologist who worked with us, played a big part in this aspect of our game. He came up with categories of personalities that we used to analyse ourselves and our opponents. It became a really effective device and helped us win some key moments in tough contests.

Jauncey designed four categories. There were Mozzies, who played just on instinct. Mozzies would never think too much; they would just go out there and do what came naturally. Andrew Symonds was a perfect example of a Mozzie. There were Enforcers, like Matthew Hayden, who wanted to be tough, aggressive and impose themselves on the opposition.

Thinkers were players who would be very well organised and structured. Thinkers needed things to be in order and under control. Finally there were Feelers, who needed to hear reinforcement, feel valued and loved. Between each category were combinations, meaning you could have, for instance, Mozzie-Feelers or Enforcer-Thinkers or Feeler-Thinkers. Before matches or series we would spend time working out which category our opponents fitted into. From there we could decide whether or not to get in their ear and what things we might say to try to distract them.

If we identified a player as an Enforcer, we knew there was no point sledging him. England's Kevin Pietersen was one we felt fitted into that category. Kevin was ego-driven and relished confrontation. Aggressive words would only fire up a batsman like Kevin. The best approach, we believed, was to go the opposite way. We would try to make him feel relaxed by having a laugh and a friendly chat. 'G'day, KP! How are you going, mate? You're batting beautifully today. Looking really good.' It raised the chance that he would lose focus for a second or two and make a mistake.

The approach to a Feeler was at the other end of the scale. You could go hard at a Feeler because you knew that his confidence was a little susceptible and he wanted to know he was doing the right thing by his team. 'You're looking pretty tight there, mate. Looks like you're putting a bit of pressure on your batting partner. Don't let your team down.' I have a bit of Feeler in me and the Queensland team, especially, knew it and would really get stuck into me. They would always be at me, saying I did not deserve to be out there, that I was letting my team down. It worked. Queensland was the one state I never scored a century against.

With a Mozzie, the best approach was to get them thinking. When a Mozzie came to the crease we would set a leg slip or some other unusual fielding position because the last thing a Mozzie wants is information going around in his mind. He just wants to be on autopilot. 'Watch out for the leg slip', you might remind the Mozzie batsman. As soon as he's thinking about the guy at leg slip he's no longer playing his natural uncluttered game. He is second-guessing himself and beginning to worry.

None of these tactics is unfair play or outside the spirit of cricket, as far as I'm concerned. They are actually very smart tactics and very relevant in a game that is a test of concentration and character. I equate them to analysing a player's technique and looking for weaknesses or chinks in their armour. If you see a weakness you are entitled to home in on it and see how the opponent responds. I see studying a player's mental technique as being as viable a tool as studying his physical technique.

Sledging has a bad name because there have been many unsavoury incidents. Certainly there is no room for personal or racial or religious abuse. But there are very clever ways to use language that come nowhere near that low level of conduct.

Steve Waugh could be vicious at times but he was also very cunning in his mind games. I remember in a game against NSW Steve came running in from slip to next to where I was standing at the crease. He ordered the fielder at point to 'just move back a bit'. He stood there for another moment, looked me in the eye and then called the fielder back in. 'Actually, no. He won't play any shots anyway.' It made me feel pretty unsettled! In the same game, Shaun Marsh was getting close to his maiden first-class hundred, Mark Waugh was bowling and Steve started saying to Shaun, 'Mate, you've done so well today. Don't throw it away now. You've been really awesome. Don't choke now.'

I am pleased to say as a proud West Australian that Steve's mind games did not pay off for the Blue Baggers that day. Shaun made 119 and I made 90. But those sledges stayed in my mind as great examples of how words can be used to try to put a batsman off without crossing the line of fair play.

Where fair play takes on a different meaning

Things boil over from time to time in international and first-class cricket. Guys are playing for their careers and livelihoods. National pride, rivalries and history between players are built up over years of hard competition. There are antagonisers, like Harbhajan Singh and Kieron Pollard and David Warner, who prompt confrontations and thrive on them. There are bullies and rascals and hotheads. It's a cauldron and guys sometimes lose control.

Junior cricket is a different proposition altogether. There is absolutely no room for attacking or abusing opponents.

Players should never be made to feel intimidated or scared. They should never be made to feel inferior or discouraged from having a go. They should be emboldened and spurred on to test their abilities, improve and enjoy playing the game. That is why I believe it's wrong to dismiss on-field banter entirely in junior games.

Talking on the field can be a positive lesson, as long as it's conducted properly. I like watching a game of kids' cricket in which the slips fielders yell encouragement to the bowler. I like hearing a wicketkeeper supporting the guys around him. I like seeing a batsman put his hand on his batting partner's shoulder between overs and urge him to not worry about the ball he just missed. When someone does something good, that player should be congratulated by his teammates. When he makes a mistake he should be encouraged to do better next time. These are lessons as valuable as anything cricket has to offer.

It's very hard to police junior cricket. But I think one golden rule could solve a lot of problems. I believe players should simply not communicate at all with opponents during a game. All their talk should be directed towards teammates. It's a black-and-white policy, which I think could help clarify the lines between what is acceptable and what is not at the junior level. It would also teach kids to focus their energies on helping their teammates rather than bringing down their opponents. There is plenty of pressure a team can build on the batsmen just by encouraging their own players. Plenty of yelling, buzzing and clapping in the field will get the batsmen thinking they are really up against it and will test them out. Talking directly to opponents can come later, when young players have had more experience and better understand its legitimate tactical uses.

The difficulty lies at the point where junior cricket and elite cricket meet. Kids will always want to copy what they see their heroes doing on TV. With so much more of the game exposed by new media and technology, that poses big obstacles. If Channel Nine's cameras zero in on an Australian player giving the batsman a mouthful it's hard to expect a young Australian kid not to want to do it too when they play the next Saturday morning. Parents, too, are left in a bind because when they see their kids copying examples of poor sportsmanship they wonder if cricket is the best option for their child. The result is that the authorities are left in the unenviable position of having to walk a tightrope between two big forces working against each other: the competitive, high-pressure international game where things sometimes boil over, and the junior game, which tries to encourage participation through the promotion of strong values and ethics.

My reasoning to parents who are concerned about poor behaviour at the elite level infiltrating junior cricket would be this: remember that players who infringe on the big stage are subjected to stricter fair play rules than ever before. There is plenty of evidence to suggest that while infringements happen from time to time they are not an acceptable part of the game and are punished quite severely. I think the fact that there are strict rules in place is a good advertisement for cricket. It shows there are consequences for irresponsible actions, an important life lesson for any youngster to learn.

Our legacy

Fair play was always important to me, not as a conscious goal but just as the ingrained way I was taught to go about everyday life. I am thankful for that because once I finished playing I came to realise how much having a good reputation was important post-cricket. It made my decision to retire easier knowing I was well regarded and had no regrets. I was able to walk away from the game on top in terms of my form and abilities but also feeling satisfied that lovers of the game felt I had played it in good spirit.

Towards the end of my career I had offers to work with companies who said they wanted to associate with me because I was seen as reliable, trustworthy and with a good name in the community. It helped me get work with Channel Nine, among other work options, enabled me to play longer in the IPL, and has opened the doors to some coaching offers that I might take up in the future.

I like to think that my example and that of Adam Gilchrist and others show that players can reach the pinnacle of cricket and also play in the right spirit. Good guys can finish on top. The founding values of our game do not need to be surrendered because of the modern super-competitive manner in which the game is played. You do not need to be nasty or continually test the boundaries of what is acceptable to be successful.

We are all custodians of the game, whether at Test level at the world's greatest grounds or fifth-grade level down at the local park. Cricket has been going for nearly 150 years and will go on well after all of us have moved on. It's our duty to conduct our playing of the game in a way that makes it that little bit better. All our legacies will live on through the game in some small way. What MS Dhoni said that day as we walked onto the ground at Chennai might have got a laugh out of the guys. But – whether he intended it or not – it was a very poignant message for our times.

LEADERSHIP

My leaders

I have had the good fortune to play under some fabulous captains who taught me so much about leadership. Each was great in his own particular way, offering diverse lessons in how to be successful in different environments through different approaches and styles.

Tom Moody at Western Australia was the first captain I had who made a big impact on me. Tom was a big strong man, a super-hard competitor and dominant personality. Tom made you really earn your respect in the team and made you always feel that the team was above the individual. He was very much about working hard and being disciplined and if you did not meet those standards he would pull you into line in no uncertain terms. Tom never held back when he wanted to get a message across. There were times under Tom when I felt quite intimidated. But one of his great skills was being very clear about what he expected from the team around him and in which direction he wanted to take us.

Ricky Ponting, as Australian captain, was less communicative in terms of his expectations. Rather, Ricky's captaincy style was to lead by example, especially in the way he trained and prepared. Ricky's work around the game's edges was inspirational. He left absolutely nothing to chance and provided a shining example, especially for younger players, to learn from and try to emulate. On the field he was the kind of leader you wanted to rally around because of his incredibly strong will to win and never-say-die attitude. You often hear about players wanting to 'win for the coach'. If there was one player I felt I wanted to win for it was Ricky.

One thing that was unusual and fairly challenging about playing under Ricky compared with other leaders was that he was a supremely gifted athlete. It was something that as a member of his team you could interpret negatively or positively. In some ways you never felt you could quite live up to Ricky's expectations just by the sheer fact that he could do things with a bat and ball no one else could. You could train for countless hours in the nets, do all sorts of work to sharpen your reflexes, try everything at your disposal, but you simply could not match him in most aspects of the game. It could feel quite deflating at times. On the other hand his remarkable abilities provided every player on the team with something to strive that little bit extra for, to really stretch themselves to their potential and bring out their best.

Michael Clarke, my next Australian team captain, led by example like Ricky but seemed to zero in more on players' physical condition. Michael demanded everyone in the team be as fit and strong as possible. He got us working like finely tuned athletes, which was a phenomenal achievement given that the Australian team already held very high standards in that area. Michael took that part of our game to a new level.

I only played under Michael for about eighteen months and much of that time, I think, was a settling-in period for him. There were a couple of things that were evident straight away. One was that Michael had a very sharp cricket mind. He understood cricket very well and always tried to take the game forward. There were times we thought we needed to score a few more runs before declaring but Michael would back our bowlers and fielders to roll our opponents. If we were chasing runs he would always give licence to the batsmen to go for it. It was a bit against the policy of the previous decade or so, when we would seem to often err on the side of caution. Michael's positivity and aggression in taking calculated risks was a refreshing and exciting change.

The other thing that was clear to me about Michael's early leadership was that he was very strict about the team being behind him. If you did not fall into line with Michael's vision you were not likely to be around for much longer. In that regard there were aspects of his leadership that were quite ruthless.

Another captain of mine who displayed some great leadership skills was Adam Gilchrist, who was outstanding at recognising players' different personalities and needs. Adam, who led the Australian Test and one-day teams when Ponting was unavailable, had great natural empathy for people and put in place programs and policies to use that talent for the team's benefit.

He would get players to open up and talk about their lives. He wanted everyone to know their teammates as people as well as cricketers. He wanted to make sure everyone was happy within the team. It really helped bring everyone together.

Adam's promotion of team spirit and camaraderie as the national team's long-term vice-captain showed on the field in the way he always stayed positive whatever the situation. Even if the opposition was 1–200, Adam would be shouting encouragement from behind the stumps, never letting things slide out of control. Off the field he was big on celebrating together and making sure everyone shared in each other's and the team's successes.

The final captain in the exceptional bunch I was lucky to play under is MS Dhoni, who was very different from the traditional Australian disciplinarian-style leader. Dhoni, my skipper at Chennai in the IPL, was so relaxed that he sometimes gave the impression that he was not very interested in what was going on around him. He was never one to reprimand you for wearing the wrong hat or being five minutes late to training, and he never spoke up in team meetings. In fact he felt meetings were a complete waste of time.

These characteristics might seem curious but I think Dhoni's incredible calmness around the group had the effect of allowing players to take ownership of their game and find their place within the side. MS was very big on personal responsibility and placed a lot of trust in players to do their job.

Above all, I think, Dhoni's style was perfect for the environment in which he worked. India is such a cricket-mad country, there is so much pressure on the players that it can be overbearing. MS would try to take away some of that strain by staying very measured and cool. He would remind players that it was just a game and they should enjoy the experience. He wanted everyone to give their all but did a great job of relieving that heavy external expectation that followed the teams he led.

Leadership beyond captaincy

The players mentioned above were all captains. But leadership is not necessarily restricted to the bloke who tosses the coin on game day. Leadership is a range of qualities and skills that can positively influence teammates to be their best and contribute to the side.

I think there are five basic attributes that form the foundation of a good leader, whether a captain, coach, manager or player.

1. **Leading from the front.** This refers to the way the player prepares and trains, performs under pressure and sets the example for others around him.
2. **Showing empathy.** This means having the ability to understand and work with different personalities.
3. **Providing clear roles and responsibilities.** This is about communicating effectively so everyone is on the same page. It is primarily the task of official leaders.
4. **Having a consistent character.** A good leader will not get swept up in the good times or the bad, but will keep a mostly even level of emotion and promote balance to those around him.
5. **Being trustworthy.** Giving people the confidence to feel they can be open and honest.

Leading from the front

In Australia, rightly or wrongly, the captain is often the best player in the team. This automatically places him in the position of setting the example. Other players will watch the way he trains and prepares, carries himself, responds to pressure, and handles the media and other duties.

The great from-the-front leaders I have seen, like Ricky and Michael, were phenomenal in setting the standard for others to follow. There is so much work to do as Australian captain, including all the official requirements beyond game day, but those two showed their players that there was no excuse for being anything other than completely ready by the time they walked out onto the ground. Ricky, particularly, had an extraordinary ability to put all the distractions to one side, pick up his bat and play with freedom and clarity.

Showing empathy

To be truly part of a team you need to be able to recognise what your teammates are going through. There are form slumps, injuries, external pressures, all sorts of events that can affect a player's state of mind. I think the best leaders are aware when a teammate is struggling.

Recognising when someone is going through a tough period opens the door to be able to help. The empathetic leader is able to say to the struggling teammate 'I've been through this before.' He might explain what he did to come out the other side or offer other ways to help address the problem. Sometimes merely asking how the teammate is feeling and listening to him a bit can help stabilise the situation and provide a base for him to work his own way back. It will at least give him confidence to know that his captain or other leaders in the team care. When things are not going well cricket can be pretty lonely. Sometimes it's nice to just have another player or even a coach come to you and say, 'I get it.'

Providing clear roles and responsibilities

Often when a player is having problems he will say, fairly or not, something like 'I don't know what's expected of me', 'I'm getting mixed messages' or 'I don't know what my role is.' On one hand a response to those statements could be 'Maybe you need to figure it out for yourself.' But on the other hand, in the really good teams I have played in and come across, it appears that everyone understands exactly what their role is. The job of a leader in this instance is to precisely outline what is expected of each player. There should be no doubt about what each team member is supposed to do to help the side, whether it's to bowl as fast as possible in short spells, bat for time, hold up an end, lead the chatter in the field or anything else.

The advantage of clearly defined roles is that if a player enters a cricket match – or any pursuit, really – concentrating on doing one or two things as well as possible, he will more than likely feel capable of succeeding because he has minimised the distractions. If you are not sure of your role or responsibilities within a team you might start to wonder about the guys who are sledging you or that you have not scored many runs lately or that the selectors are watching. It's easy to be weighed down with thoughts about things other than the immediate task. A good leader will help lessen the obstacles by providing transparency and direction.

Having a consistent character

It is very tempting for any member of a team to go right over the top when the team has a good win. It is easy at such times to make big statements or get overconfident and celebrate really hard. By the same token if the team has a disappointing loss or is going through a tough time there is the danger of falling into a hole and becoming negative. At times like these, having a stable character at the helm is very important. Leaders who treat ups and downs as little troughs rather than big speed bumps will influence those around them to stay even-tempered.

Ricky was very good at keeping level. You could hardly ever tell if he was having personal struggles or whether the team was enduring a good or bad run. He stayed the same bloke all the time. Often we revere a player because he wears his heart on his sleeve. But the last thing you want in a captain is for him to be overly emotional as he rides the bumpy waves of performance and results.

Being trustworthy

Most players have people outside of the team environment they can confide in and bounce ideas off. However, having an authority within the team whom they can trust and discuss their thoughts with openly and honestly raises the sense of camaraderie within the group. It allows the player to feel there is a genuine bond between him and his leader or leaders. Having a trustworthy figurehead promotes harmony, respect and belief among the entire team.

Leadership through thick and thin

In November 2014, Michael Clarke was trying to overcome injury and get the Australian side ready to host India after losing to Pakistan in the Middle East. Not only was the team looking to bounce back, but Michael had plenty of personal challenges going on, including a well-publicised disagreement with Cricket Australia over how he should recover in order to play in the Test matches. Suddenly and tragically everything came to a halt when our little mate Phillip Hughes was struck while playing in a match at the Sydney Cricket Ground.

Michael's display of leadership throughout that awful time was exemplary. He managed to find ways to support so many people while balancing his own desperate feelings of shock and sadness. He spent just about all his time at the hospital with Phil and Phil's family, helped out his teammates and became the focal point for the media after Phil left us.

It was not an event that Michael could have prepared for. Certainly nothing like this had happened before in any of our careers. Rather, I think, Michael's conduct showed his natural ability to lead and how far he had developed as a manager of people.

Quite often as international cricketers we put up shields and try to keep our true selves hidden from the outside world. But Michael showed a genuinely human side throughout the ordeal. There was no bravado, no protecting himself from scrutiny or criticism; he just laid it all out there. It demonstrated to his teammates that he cared deeply about them and it gave permission, in a way, for everyone else – right across the country – to put down their guard and let their true emotions flow.

The basis of Michael's leadership during that time was to organise his priorities. Admittedly it was pretty clear-cut – a disaster had taken place and there was no space for anything else in those few days afterwards, either practically or emotionally. Nonetheless I think a very important aspect of the good leadership Michael displayed was his ability to pick out what was most important in those shattering moments. Michael put everything to the side, including his own struggles, and concentrated on helping Phillip's family, friends and teammates. He then addressed the nation on behalf of everyone close to Phillip. I was very impressed with how he handled the whole situation.

A simple singular focus

It is impossible to compare the Phillip Hughes tragedy with anything else. But I think the point about being able to recognise what is important is very relevant to leadership and captaincy. A great example of prioritising to great effect came from Ricky Ponting after the loss of the Ashes in 2005, when it felt as though the world had ended.

I was not yet part of the Test side but I remember the atmosphere in the community after the team's return was one of doom and gloom. We had lost to the Poms after a long stretch of holding the Ashes, and people were worried that the Australian team had passed its peak and the media was baying for blood. In that environment we had to somehow prepare for the Australian summer, which was to begin with three one-dayers and a Test match against the World XI.

We had a team meeting in the hotel before the one-day series started and I remember it so clearly because of the effective message Ricky conveyed. Recognising that we needed to start this new series on a strong footing, Ricky talked about the importance of eliminating outside influences and distractions. He reassured us there was no need to change too much about what we had been doing, except for one thing – he felt that towards the end of the Ashes the team had not been training to its full potential.

It is remarkable how powerful simple directives can be when events around you feel complex. We could have talked all about aspects of our game as individuals and as a team, we could have analysed tactics we had used and all the what-ifs. There were so many things we could have tried to pick apart and fix. But Ricky knew that to do all that would have only clouded the situation. It would have made things harder and more complex. He believed the best way to overcome our predicament was to zero in on one area of our game that we could do better and put all our energy into it.

After that meeting every player refocused on his training and preparation. Each team member thought about what he could do just that little bit more efficiently in his practice. The straightforwardness of Ricky's advice helped us stay tight and strong, shut out the noise from the critics and set about getting our game back to its best. It worked really well. We won all three limited-overs matches comfortably and then sealed the Test match by 210 runs.

Leadership in a crisis

Most people would think that times of crisis are the critical moments for leaders to stand up and be counted: when the storm clouds are closing in it's up to Captain Courageous to take charge and save the day. However, I don't think it's necessarily so black and white.

Good leadership is evident no matter what the situation. It is evident in good times and bad. When things are going well it's vital for the captain, coach or other leaders in the group to make sure people are getting along, standards are not slipping and that guys are not getting ahead of themselves. I have been in teams where we have won so many games and series that complacency became a real danger. We started to train less intensely, celebrated too hard and took things for granted. We needed to be pulled back into line by the captain or other respected figures within the group.

If a leader performs his tasks during the good times, dealing with the bad times should not be as hard as it sounds. The trust and stability he needs to impart during the crisis have been built up already. He has been approachable and available. He has set a good example and given the people around him the feeling of consistency. Players will listen and trust the leader when he says, 'OK, boys, what we need to do now that we're in a spot of bother is just concentrate on A, B and C. Disregard all the stuff that's going on around us and let's just do what we have to do to get out of this.' It's why people listened to Ricky's directives in that meeting after the 2005 Ashes.

Similar attributes are required to deal with players going through crises off the field. All sorts of situations come up in groups of people. Sporting teams are in many ways representative of society. There will be some guys who fall off the rails or do stupid things no matter what they have been taught, how good an example has been set for them or how stable their environment is.

As in society, I don't think it's fair to simply point the finger elsewhere when someone does the wrong thing. It's impossible for the captain to monitor everything every player in his team is doing. It's important that individuals realise their responsibility to themselves and their teammates. But there is definitely a place for leadership to step in when players get into trouble away from the game, whether it's to sit down with them and offer assistance or advice, meet with team management to discuss positive ways forward or even, if appropriate, publicly back the players.

Knowing each and every player

One of the biggest tests for a leader is to understand that players at different stages of their careers have different requirements. A player with years of experience might not have a great need to see a leader setting a good example in his preparation and training, as he already knows what is necessary and has proven he can live up to those demands. A player just starting out would probably gain a lot from such a leadership style.

One of the toughest challenges for Michael Clarke so early in his Test captaincy career was that, because he was heading a side with several inexperienced players, he was required to demonstrate so many of the qualities that comprise a good leader. He had to set a good example. He had to show empathy and make new teammates feel at ease. He had to give clear directions so players could concentrate on their tasks. He had to be consistent, stable and trustworthy. It was a very tall order for any captain, especially one who was quite new to the job.

Adding to Michael's task, he also had to recognise that players can have different needs even if they are at the same level of experience. You could have two nineteen-year-olds come into the team and have one be self-assured and the other insecure. Similarly, you could have two thirty-year-olds, each feeling differently about his role, his current form, the external pressures he is experiencing and a range of other factors. All these players will want to be spoken to in different ways and will respond to different messaging. It is up to the leaders to work out what the best approach is with each team member. There's not one uniform rule for players of different ages or stages.

One tactic that seemed to work quite well in the Australian team was delegating leadership duties to people within groups. It was never an explicit policy but there tended to be a structure among the bowlers and among the batsmen. These days, for instance, Mitchell Johnson enjoys the unofficial role he has in guiding the younger bowlers in the side, imparting his knowledge, being someone they can trust and setting standards for them to follow. It's the kind of role that Glenn McGrath used to fulfil for Mitch. The more official mentor system the Australian team used was another example of how leadership duties could be spread among the group, helping out those who needed guidance and providing the mentors with a new way they could contribute.

My captaincy experiences

I had the great honour of captaining the Australian team a handful of times. Unfortunately I did not have much success. But, as in every experience, there were lessons to be learned and I tried to understand where I had gone wrong so I could do better if the opportunity came up again.

The first game I was at the helm of was a one-dayer in Kuala Lumpur, Malaysia. It was a DLF Cup match against the West Indies, which we lost by three wickets. I didn't worry myself too much about it because it was a one-off game in a pretty obscure tournament. However, the second time I captained Australia was different. It was for a three-game series against New Zealand, in New Zealand, that we ended up losing 3–0.

During my periods as captain of Western Australia and Northamptonshire my philosophy was always to be careful not to put myself above the players or make them feel uncomfortable or undervalued. I wanted everyone to be engaged and encouraged. But I still managed to be assertive in my communication and tactics. When I look back on those games against New Zealand it becomes obvious to me that there were stages when I was indecisive and did not show the kind of conviction I had previously.

Filling in for another captain is not easily done. It was not my team, it was Ricky Ponting's team, and I was just holding the fort while he was rested. It was always going to be a hard ask, slotting into captaining a side that had been shaped by someone else's beliefs and standards. But that was only a small excuse for letting the decision-making process get away from me.

Several times, I remember, we would be heading down one avenue but I would let myself get talked into taking a different one. I would then bounce ideas off someone else only to reassess the whole situation and go down yet another path. One area in which I needed to show more confidence was setting fields. I always thought it important as a captain to talk to the bowlers about what they were trying to do and support them with field placings. I wanted my bowlers to feel backed up as they searched for ways to dismiss the batsmen. Against New Zealand I gave too much leeway for the bowlers to dictate. It was fine to listen to what they thought or wanted but, ultimately, setting the field is the captain's responsibility and I needed to take that responsibility on.

I remember one situation when Shane Watson was bowling. I wanted a fielder back at long-on but he was adamant that long-on come up. I gave in and, sure enough, the ball kept flying over the mid-on fielder. I wish I had been more direct. I needed to put my foot down and take charge rather than be tentative and worry about upsetting people.

One thing that chastening experience taught me was that good captaincy takes time to develop. Experience comes from making mistakes and learning from them. It's like anything, the more you do it the more you learn and the better you become. In that regard it would have been nice to have further opportunities to lead the side and see if, by building up a backlog of experience with the team, aspects of my captaincy would have improved.

I better understood this obstacle when I became captain of Sydney Thunder. In my first year as Thunder skipper I suffered from the same problem as when I led the Australian team – I held back too much and did not genuinely feel invested in my convictions. I did not have enough of a handle on how the system ran and the inner workings of Cricket NSW. I did not know most of the players and was uncertain about how I should interact with them. When I returned for my second year leading the team I felt very different. I was much more familiar with the players and the structure around the team and felt a much greater sense of ownership of my role as skipper. It led to me being more decisive and genuinely taking charge.

The missing generation

I think young players today have a unique opportunity to develop qualities that could make them great leaders down the track. The reason is that there seems to be a missing generation of players in club cricket. It sounds like an unhealthy situation for the game but, if looked at as the glass half full, it says to me that young guys have the chance to take an increased leadership role in their respective teams.

When I look back on my early days playing A-grade cricket in Perth one thing that stands out to me is that I was one of a very small number of players in the side who were really young. The rest of the team consisted of guys in their mid to late twenties and early thirties who had played years of club cricket and had a wealth of knowledge to pass along. They were the players who showed you the ropes and shaped your view of the game and how it should be played.

It was a hard school. I remember the older guys using us younger ones as whipping boys. But that sort of treatment left you in no doubt about the work that was required to get ahead of the pack. I found it quite motivating and I wonder if I would have got as far as I did in my career without that environment as part of my background.

It seems to me that the seniority structure in club cricket is gone. In fact it feels that the structure has been turned upside down – teams commonly feature maybe one or two older guys and the majority are youngsters. There are a few reasons why a generation of players is missing but probably none as obvious as the Greg Chappell–inspired policy of making the state Second XI competition nearly exclusively the domain of under-twenty-five-year-olds.

The Futures League concept was, in my view – and in the view of many senior players in Australian cricket – a big mistake. Our concerns were proven right when it became apparent that an exodus had begun of good-quality grade players who were around their peak. They walked away from the game as they realised that the door on a possible start in the Sheffield Shield had been slammed shut in favour of young hotshots.

Their departures created a void that has filtered right through the grades in clubs around the country, extracting a great whack of the nation's cricketing know-how. To their credit, Cricket Australia heeded the concerns of current and past players, which were expressed in a huge State of the Game report in 2014, and reversed the policy. But I believe the knock-on effect of that policy could last years.

What does it mean? Well, it's difficult to learn about the game from those who have experienced it if they're not around to talk about it. But we need to make the most of the circumstances and

I think there could be a silver lining. The opportunity for young cricketers to take ownership of their teams has probably never been greater. Young players in grade teams have a chance to run their teams the way they want. They can step up to the plate in terms of taking charge and displaying leadership in a way they could never have done with the oldies in control. By taking a leading role in their team at an earlier stage younger players can create a real culture of togetherness, learning through experience the lessons of team-building and comradeship.

When I was a young player coming through I had no say in how things should be done. I sat in the corner, kept quiet and hoped no one would make fun of me. Today's young players can get together, talk to their peers and work out for themselves ways to create a team environment that suits them. How do we want the team to be run? How do we want to be seen? How do we want to play? What do we stand for as a group? They have a chance to create new club cultures that could last well into the future.

Ownership and communication within a team creates well-rounded people and players. Instead of just copying what Tom Moody does or what Justin Langer does – as I did when I was starting out – players can ask questions more freely, evaluate the answers and consider what might be right or wrong for them. They can truly take ownership if they are willing and do not sit idly by waiting for their turn to take control. That is a huge positive for the future leadership of Australian cricket.

COACHING

Man in the mirror

At my very first Cricket Australia camp Steve Waugh invited the revered rugby league coach Wayne Bennett to address the squad. Most of the guys were excited but I could not for the life of me understand what a rugby league coach could offer the Australian cricket team. My impression of rugby league was that it was a game played by massive blokes who could just about run through brick walls. It was all crash, bash and smash. I thought it had no relation to me or the way I went about my cricket.

To this day Wayne's speech remains one of the most inspirational addresses I have ever heard. It was nothing to do with crash and bash motivation. Wayne said during his speech that riling up a team to physically belt the opposition was only useful for maybe a handful of minutes in a game. After that, he said, motivation had to come from within.

Wayne's working title for this approach was 'the man in the mirror'. What he meant was that every player needed to look himself in the eye and answer the questions 'Did I give myself the best chance of being successful today? Did I prepare as well as I possibly could? Did I put in every bit of effort possible to ensure I performed at my best?' A successful athlete is able to look at the man in the mirror – himself – and be completely honest about the way he goes about reaching his goals.

To hear a highly successful coach say that desire should emanate from inside the athlete, rather than from mentors and other outside factors, really struck home with me. I thought Wayne's concept was spot-on. Coaches can try all sorts of tactics to get players to be switched on, to work as a team, to execute well and to attain the many other requirements for achieving highly. But only the player has the ability to answer for certain whether he has ticked all the boxes leading up to that point. A coach can only do so much. The athlete must take ultimate responsibility for performance.

My coaches

Wayne Bennett challenged me to review my mode of becoming the best cricketer I could be. He also got me thinking about what I should expect from coaches and mentors. Yes, ultimately the buck stops with the player. But a good coach can help set aspects of the pathway in place for an athlete and the team.

I see the role of a coach as helping to create an environment that is conducive to good team play. The way to achieve this is to ensure that each player feels they belong and their personality is encouraged to come out. A coach can achieve this by learning how to identify what makes different types of people tick and being able to bring together a range of characters to work together harmoniously and effectively. More practically, the coach's job is to provide any resource possible for every player to be able to get the best out of himself.

Wayne was one of several coaches, captains and leaders who over the years made an impact on me. I feel privileged to have learned from some of the best in the business. Each of these coaches has offered different perspectives and lessons to heed, going right back to the start when I began playing cricket at Whitfords Junior Cricket Club.

Bob Mitchell was the under 12s coach at Whitfords and I can thank Bob for helping lay the foundation for everything that came afterwards. I was a very little kid for my age, lacked power and had few if any shots in my repertoire. Far from telling me I might be better off taking up another sport, Bob encouraged me to concentrate on making sure my technique was sound. 'Don't worry', he said. 'When you start growing and catching up to the other boys, the big hitters will be getting out to the good bowlers and you'll be out there batting and batting because you'll have a nice solid technique and defence.'

It was a great piece of advice for two reasons. It gave me something to concentrate on instead of worrying about being inferior to the bigger kids. Also, Bob was right. Cementing a good technique from that early age really did help me later on when the standard of cricket became harder. As I rose through the ranks I had the confidence of knowing that years of hard technical work were behind me and I could start to show how much I had developed. I was actually able to bat for hours and hours and it felt great.

The other really important thing about the way Bob coached the team was that he made sure we always had fun. An example was that at the end of each training session everyone had to catch one high ball before we were allowed to go home. Bob would set the scene for you. 'OK, it's Australia versus the West Indies', he might say. 'Viv Richards skies one and Hussey's underneath it. Can he catch it? He can! What a catch! Hussey's won the game for Australia!' You would go running around high-fiving your teammates and carrying on. You would go home in a positive frame of mind and look forward to coming back for the next training session. Bob was really good at mixing the technical points of cricket development with the enjoyment side of the game.

My club coach at Wanneroo, Ian Kevan, was the next big influence on my career. Ian was a real lover of cricket and willing to put in a huge amount of time and effort for those young guys who showed a strong keenness to advance. Ian seemed to take a personal interest in me and genuinely wanted to do whatever he could to help me become a better batsman.

Ian was dependable and generous. He provided drill after drill in the nets, getting me grooving bat swings hour after hour. It was unbelievable how many underarm throws he gave me. Ian was big on technique and mechanics, as Bob had been, and wanted to see me reach perfection in my batting. He never cut corners. He just gave and gave and gave.

Ian was the first coach I had who took an interest in my life away from the game. Apart from helping with the huge volume of training, he wanted to know how my studies were going, how my family life was, what other things I was doing outside of cricket. We caught up socially and played games of golf. He became something of a father figure to me, especially during the summer, as my dad was more into football than cricket. Dad used to joke about it being time to hand me over to Ian whenever summer was upon us.

When I was about seventeen Ian decided I was ready to play A-grade. He identified me as someone who could push on and, while it was nice to know he had that much confidence in me, I was terrified of facing some of the bowlers who were around at that level. It was almost as though Ian had more faith in me than I had in myself. He was and still is a strong backer of mine and remains a great friend.

I felt lucky to have one Ian Kevan in my life. But later on when I was playing at Northamptonshire I became doubly lucky to have another great mentor come into my life. Bob Carter was a sweet man, a really caring soul whose belief was that if you were happy and content off the field you would give yourself a better chance of doing well on it. He really lived up to that theory, always making sure Amy and I had everything we needed to feel settled.

Aside from making sure everything tangible was in place, Bob filled me with plenty of belief. He was the coach who told me I would need a manager when I started playing for Australia one day. I laughed at him. I thought he was joking. But he was serious. He truly believed I would have an international career and, as unrealistic as his comments seemed to me, they gave me that little inkling that maybe, just maybe, it could happen.

Before I came across Bob in England I worked under Wayne Clark at Western Australia. Wayne was not my first coach in the state system but he was the one I spent the most time with and had perhaps the most influence on me. Wayne was a very relaxed character – some would say too relaxed – but his main philosophy on the game was a very important one. He was very big on the idea that cricket was not just about the individual, it was about everyone working together.

Around the time of Wayne's stint we had terrific players in the WA side but were not having much success. It was because some of the players were more concerned about their own back-yards than the fate of the team as a whole. Wayne was very good at conveying the message that if you wanted individual achievements they would be much more likely to occur if the team was performing well as a group.

Wayne's message sank in. When he started out we had no one in the Australian team. Once his mantra got through we won back-to-back Sheffield Shields and made a couple of other finals. It started an era of dominance for WA in which a stack of players, including Jo Angel, Brendon Julian, Tom Moody, Justin Langer and Adam Gilchrist were picked for Australia. I think some of the credit for their progress can be attributed to Wayne.

When I first played for Australia John Buchanan was the coach. John was something of a polarising figure among the players and the public. One common perception was that, given the players he had at his disposal – Gilchrist, Warne, McGrath, Hayden and so on – anyone could have coached that team and had success. But I could not agree with that view and do not think it was a fair reflection of John's abilities and what he brought to the table.

John might not have been all that helpful with hands-on tuition but he was a genius at identifying what made each player tick and motivating each according to his personality and character. He knew how to light the fuse within a player and spur him to keep forging ahead even in a side that kept winning game after game. He would take on Matthew Hayden because he knew that was what Matthew needed to fire up. Same, in some ways, with Shane Warne. With me he would offer encouragement and make sure I had every training device known to man at my disposal because he knew they were the conditions that made me feel my best and play my best.

Recognising the remarkable talent among the group, John set the bar extremely high. He believed the players were capable of extraordinary things and challenged them to push beyond previous boundaries. He wanted to see our team take the game to levels that even we doubted were possible. What other coach would have told his team in 2006 that they should aim to score 400 runs in a one-dayer? In a team of big stars and bigger egos, John's intellect, calming style and clever management skills fitted the bill perfectly.

The next national coach we had was Tim Nielsen, whose incredible work ethic and deep passion for the team really struck me. Tim would throw ball after ball in the nets all day and then turn up the next day and do it all again. His willingness to strive intensely and relentlessly was a great example for the players and set a good standard within the team.

There were times Tim and I had disagreements, most notably around the 2011 World Cup when I was coming back from a hamstring injury and he and the selectors decided every player had to be fit before the first game. I found him stubborn and difficult to deal with at that time. But what it proved to me was that Tim had the courage to make tough decisions, stick to his guns and back himself in enforcing them.

Tim was a genuinely good bloke, a real student of the game who relished playing an important role for the Australian cricket team. Tim gave you the impression he would do anything for you and anything for the cause. I found it quite inspiring to think there was someone in the trenches with me, feeling every shot, every struggle, every effort.

Mickey Arthur followed Tim. Mickey's coaching, in my opinion, was extremely organised and well managed. He would get a bit overly nervous at times during games. But the quality of the training he provided, the facilities we used, the set-up and organisation of the sessions were probably the best I ever encountered.

One of Mickey's best attributes was that he had a great ability to delegate to his support staff. He oversaw everything but allowed the batting, bowling and fielding assistants plenty of rope to bring their skills into the team surroundings and work the way they wanted. He showed trust in the support staff, which helped the players to trust them too.

At Chennai Super Kings, Stephen Fleming always impressed me with his calmness, organisation and control. He had strong opinions about how the game should be played but also demonstrated a willingness to listen and consider others' suggestions.

Stephen was very big on players taking responsibility for their own preparation and performance but made sure all the resources were available for us to be able to play our best.

Stephen added an interesting and quite modern element to his coaching in that he viewed his role holistically. To him, being the head coach was not just about leading a group of cricketers. He believed it was about understanding and dealing with the entire structure of a club. He realised whom he needed to have a good working relationship with to be able to keep the team functioning at its optimum. At Chennai, for instance, he identified MS Dhoni as someone he needed to have a strong link with because any hint of trouble with Dhoni would leave the team split, not to mention probably leave Stephen jobless. He also kept a strong link with the hierarchy of club owners, massaging egos and playing the political game cleverly to ensure that he had everything he needed to coach the team the way he wanted.

Ex-players as coaches

The former Sri Lanka captain Mahela Jayawardene rang me a while ago to ask if I would be interested in being an assistant coach of Sri Lanka with a view to taking over as head coach a few months further down the track. A week later the ex-India batsman VVS Laxman asked me if I would be interested in coaching India. My initial answer to both of them was no because at the time I did not want to be on the road ten months a year; I wanted to be at home with my family and make up for some lost time from the previous few years. But, probably more relative to them, I said to each that I did not think I was ready to become the head coach of an international cricket team.

VVS accepted that I was not interested because of family reasons. But he would not accept my feeling that I was not up to standard for a job like that. 'You have played the game very well for a long time, you know what needs to be done, you shouldn't doubt yourself', he said. I replied that coaching individuals within a team is one thing and perhaps I could do that right now. But, I said, these days coaching is not just about coaching players. It's about dealing with boards, sponsors, business owners, investors, officials, all sorts of people outside the team environment. It's a very complex job that requires numerous skills that have little or nothing to do with cricket.

Again, VVS disagreed. He said that guys with our level of experience had more understanding of the ins and outs of the game than just about anyone. It got me thinking that maybe you do not need to go off and do all sorts of courses and tick all the official boxes. Maybe just having played for so long ingrains in a long-serving former player the knowledge required to take on all that is necessary to be a good coach.

The question of whether former players make the best coaches is very hard to answer. I think there are exceptions to the rule both ways, meaning there is no correct response. I had always thought that you did not need to be a former cricketer to be a good coach. I have had some terrific coaches who did not play the game at a very high standard. John Buchanan did not play for Australia, nor did Ian Kevan. But there are certainly some advantages to having played at the top level.

Apart from having observed and gained some understanding of the official and administrative requirements of the job, the big advantage for former players is that they have realistic empathy with what elite cricketers go through. They understand the tension, the scrutiny, the pressure. They can relate when a player is out of form. They can comprehend what it's like to have the media bearing down on you. They understand the highs and lows in a way that cannot be taught from a textbook or by doing a diploma.

But the rule of ex-players being at an advantage as coaches may not always ring true. I have wondered how, for instance, Greg Chappell could have empathy for players given the immense talent he had in his heyday as Australia's best batsman. Greg went through one or two bad patches in his career but overall he was a dominating batsman, perhaps the best of his generation. The game seemed to come so easily to him. Is it possible for someone of Chappell's calibre to truly understand and appreciate the struggles of a battler like me or Chris Rogers or any number of other players?

I think my conclusion to the question of high-performing ex-players as coaches is that you do not have to have been a great player to become a great coach. There are plenty of examples of average cricketers going on to become fine coaches, offering various qualities to their sides that have nothing to do with having been able to play the game particularly well. However those who have ridden the wave all the way in international cricket will more often than not come into a coaching role with certain aspects of the job already embedded into their knowledge.

Coaching different cultures

As the cricket world continues to become globalised by Twenty20 the prevalence of foreign coaches will increase. There are already many examples of foreign coaches who have led international sides – Geoff Lawson at Pakistan, Mickey Arthur in Australia, Duncan Fletcher coaching India, John Dyson at the West Indies, among others – but T20 will take this phenomenon to much greater levels.

Coaching a side containing players from a different culture or several different cultures presents challenges beyond the usual demands of mentoring a team. I think there are good lessons to be learned from coaches who have best managed the task and I count former South Africa batsman Gary Kirsten's stint coaching India as one of the most impressive examples.

What Gary did so well was that, instead of trying to impose his beliefs and background on the Indian team, he made a conscious effort to learn about Indian culture and incorporate it into the way he coached the side. It was a clever move because that approach is much more achievable than the other way around – that is, expecting the players and hierarchy around the team to adapt to your cultural background.

There are some philosophies that are universal, such as having a good work ethic, respect for the game and recognising the importance of team spirit. You have to be firm in following your beliefs on the way certain things should be done. But when coaching a team whose cultural heritage is different from yours it is essential to be open and accepting of different ways of looking at the same things. You must be willing to adapt to what you are confronted with. It can be a daunting challenge.

Kirsten was well received by the Indian team whereas Greg Chappell had a much harder time during his stint in charge of the Indian side. From talking to some of the young Indian guys I have played IPL with, Greg had very strong ideas about the way he wanted the team to operate and many of the players were right behind him. The problem was, they said, he did not have a culturally sensitive way of conveying his vision and implementing his messages. Both Gary and Greg may have been chasing the same outcomes but Gary had more success because of his sensitivity to the cultural differences he had to contend with.

Some might argue that presently a team like the West Indies could do with a cultural change in their leadership. It seems that a disciplinarian coach – a straight-shooter who could set a few things in order, reintroduce some discipline and spirit within the side – would help promote their resurrection. But I do not think that would work. The West Indian way of life is predominantly laid-back. I do not think they would buy into a coach from outside trying to belt them into shape. If you wanted them to work harder the challenge would be to find a way to inspire them to want to work harder. I don't know what the answer is, but implementing a style of coaching that had no relation to the national culture would not achieve the desired result. Perhaps someone with the personality skills of John Buchanan would come closest to making an impact in such a tricky environment.

Coaches for the new era

I believe the future of coaching will lean increasingly towards the Stephen Fleming–Paddy Upton method. Earlier in the book I talked about the way Paddy, when he was preparing to take over as Sydney Thunder coach in 2014, suggested to me that we have no support staff at all. He wanted to buck the current trend and see how players would react to being given much more autonomy and power to decide the fate of their team. His theory, which was based on research he had done in business environments, centred on the concept of increased player responsibility and accountability.

Like Paddy, Stephen has stressed that the changing cricket world will leave players with a greater obligation to run their own show with the coaches spending more time supervising, working with overarching team issues and dealing with club hierarchy. The days of big rev-up sessions and coaches imposing their authority are fading, replaced by more managerial duties and more involvement in the business side of running a club.

For coaches of groups that spend entire seasons together playing state or international cricket, technical know-how and motivational skills will still be very important. The skills of people like Buchanan in understanding how to bring out the best in different types of people, Wayne Clark in promoting teamwork, Tim Nielsen's work ethic and Mickey Arthur's organisational skills will be vital. But as T20 continues to grow there will be a shift.

The change in the primary role of coaches will not mean their job is any less important than it once was. Players taking ownership is not a green light for coaches to sit back, relax and let things take their own course. The coach needs to be the observer and take control if something appears to be going wrong. He needs to still have his pillars that he stands by. If the players are not adhering to those pillars the coach must speak up. The coach's ethos and values should still filter through the team.

It will not be easy. Fleming has often talked about the challenges he has faced trying to gel a side in which some guys have just come from, say, four months playing in Australia, and others from a series in another part of the world. Players arrive in various physical conditions, in ranging form, from different environments, and they turn up in dribs and drabs, sometimes right up until the day before the opening game. Often it's complete chaos but Stephen would accept it for what it was and make it come together at the right time.

The key is to assess what is best for each individual rather than the whole team. It plays out with some guys sitting out training sessions, others being given space for recovery or just time away from team meetings or functions. At the 2015 IPL, Captain Dhoni literally turned up the day before the first game. It would be unheard of in traditional cricket. But in T20 it is entirely understandable and part of what the coach has to adapt to. It is a different world we live in now, without doubt.

Coaching kids

Being a dad nowadays and seeing my son playing in2CRICKET, I must admit, I sometimes become a bit frustrated. It appears to me that these nine- and ten-year-olds learn very little, if anything, about the game and are rarely challenged or encouraged to try harder. With no goals to achieve or stimulation coming from playing, it becomes boring for them.

Instead of having fifteen kids lined up to do a fielding drill, for which fourteen are waiting in a line for minutes at a time for their turn, I think the aim must be to keep as many kids as possible involved in the game at once. All kids want to do at that young age is throw balls, hit shots and run around. The aim must be to get everyone doing something, whether it's having a bat, a bowl, throwing at stumps or taking catches. Make it engaging and interesting. Keep it light and fast.

Once kids are enjoying being involved, there is space to begin offering them snippets of guidance on skills. There is nothing wrong with teaching a child to hold a bat with the proper grip. Or how to follow through with a straight bat. Or to keep their body upright when delivering a ball. They can start also learning about respecting teammates, coaches and opponents. Learning the basic elements of the game does not have to be a chore. If kids are taught to enjoy the process of learning – to enjoy seeing themselves get better at something – it's a great lesson for the following years.

As kids grow into their teens it can be time to see if individual youngsters respond well to pushing the discipline and dedication side of the game. Some early teenagers might be ready to start taking on information about the mental aspects of cricket, such as keeping focus and competing over longer periods of time. They might be ready to start thinking about how they prepare physically and mentally.

Through the early and mid teens probably the most important lesson is to start understanding what it is to be part of a team. Everyone wants to take all the wickets and score all the runs. Kids want the attention that comes from being a standout. But there comes a point where children can start moving away from that desire towards finding satisfaction in performing well as a group and seeing your teammates have individual success. Coaches can begin explaining that if Johnny takes three wickets and Jimmy scores 30 runs, we all have a better chance of winning the game. Next week maybe you will take wickets or score runs. These are lessons for life, not just cricket.

As kids get into their late teens those with promise might start thinking about career options in the game. But, whereas once all a young player dreamed about was playing Test cricket for Australia, increasingly coaches and other mentoring figures will have youngsters saying to them 'I want to play Twenty20 all around the world and make lots of money', or something to that effect. My view is, if that is what they want to do there is no point in discouraging them. The best response is to help them work out a pathway to achieving that goal.

At the moment the most common pathway to the top of the T20 tree is not all that different to that of earning a baggy green. Consistently good performances in club cricket might raise the possibility of a call-up to state cricket. Dominating performances at state level can lead to playing for Australia. Pretty much anyone who has reached international level will be on the radar of T20 teams and have the opportunity to play in competitions beyond national duties.

While playing for Australia is still the most effective way to be noticed by T20 teams, it is no longer the only way. The big difference between the earliest days of the short game and today is that outstanding form in state cricket can lead to an exclusively T20 career. It is possible to bypass the extremely difficult step of playing for Australia. Good returns, particularly in limited-overs cricket, can capture the attention of Big Bash

League (BBL) teams, and from there avenues may open up in the IPL and other T20 leagues around the world. It is an exciting development that opens the door to so many more players.

But more opportunities do not necessarily mean the competition for spots will become any easier. However different the end goal might be for new generations of cricketers, I think a coach should always impress on young players that there is no substitute for hard work. The foundation of all success – whether playing Test cricket for Australia or BBL for Sydney Thunder – is the willingness to commit to becoming the best cricketer you can be. There is no future in the game without being able to outperform the vast number of people vying for those positions. I would encourage coaches to instil in youngsters the belief that anything is possible but also to explain that there are countless others who are working extremely hard to achieve the exact same goal.

Having presented all these guidelines I would qualify my advice by saying this: not all kids want to become the best cricketer they can – and that is fine. It's a very important point for coaches to be aware of and one that, as a parent, I have thought about a lot.

When I was growing up, all I wanted to do was play for Australia. I was almost obsessive about doing everything possible to advance up the ladder and reach my ultimate goal. But for every guy like me, there must have been hundreds of others who had no genuine desire to make cricket their career. There were those who were maybe happier going to the beach than going to training after school or work. There must have been many who played cricket on a Saturday because it was fun and they looked forward to having a beer with their mates after the game. Maybe they still wanted to do well and contribute to their team. But whereas I would go to the nets day after day to continue trying to improve, their priority might have been to study medicine or accountancy or a trade.

The point is, it is essential for coaches to always be aware that cricket, above all, should be about enjoyment, whatever the end game. Children playing any sport should never feel pressured to do anything they feel uncomfortable with. Some kids just want to be outdoors, running around with their mates. They do not care about scoring more runs than anyone else or winning as many games as possible. They should never be pushed into a corner by overenthusiastic coaches. They should be allowed the freedom to enjoy the game of cricket however they please.